•R.M.S. TITANIC•

THE GREATEST
DISASTERS
OF THE 20th CENTURY

Frances Kennett

Marshall Cavendish·London & New York

Pictures supplied by:
Associated Press: 30 (inset), 55, 58/9, 69T, 72/3B, 81, 84/5C, 85BR, 109, 111, 117T, 129T, 130
Australian Information Service: 110
Jim Bamber: 28/9 (Reference supplied by Patrick Stephens Limited)
Barnaby's: 14B, 32T, 33T
British Museum: 10, 11, 13
California Historical Society, San Francisco: 18/19, 23T, 151
Camera Press: 90/91, 99, 143B
Colorific: 86, 100
Daily Telegraph: 91B, 93TR
Flight International: 48/9
Fox Photos: 88
Terry Hand: 67
Harland & Wolff, Belfast: 27TR, 27BR
High Commissioner for New Zealand: 72T, 72C
Illustrated London News: 6/7, 27L, 32B, 36/7, 38/9, 40, 52/3T, 56, 71
David Jefferis: 15B, 23B
Keystone: 8/9, 14C, 78B, 79, 80T, 80BL, 80BR, 85T, 89, 97, 101T, 112, 122/3, 124/5, 127, 131
David Lees/Life Magazine © Time Inc. 1975: 100
Marvin Lichtner: 91T
London Express News & Feature Service: 84L
Manchette/Gamma/John Hillelson Agency: 120, 121B
Matador Press: 101B
Metropolitan Museum of Art: 47 Bequest of Mrs. H. O. Havemeyer 1929: The H. O. Havemeyer Collection
Mirrorpic: 78T
Mondadoripress: 15T
NASA: 106B
Odham's Press: 33B
Paris Match: 113, 114, 116/7BC, 118, 128, 129B
Photri: 104, 132, 133T, 133B, 145
Picturepoint: 121T
Popperfoto: 26, 50, 51, 52/3B, 62/3, 76/7T, 82/3, 92/3C, 96, 106TR, 116T, 119, 134T, 141B
Press Association: 42, 43, 46, 141T
Radio Times Hulton Library: 21, 25, 34, 35, 41B, 44/45, 57, 61
Rank Organisation: 30/1, 31 (inset) Stills from the film 'A Night to Remember', courtesy of Rank Organisation
Snark International: 12
Terence Spencer/Colorific: 86
St. Maur Sheil: 92/3L
Sunday Times: 94
Syndication International: 2/3, 136/7, 138/9, 140T, 140B, 143T
United Press International: 64/5, 65R, 68, 69B, 102, 103, 107T, 144, 146T, 146B, 147, 148T, 148B, 148/9T, 148/9B
US Hurricane Research Project/Diana Wylie Limited: 106TL, 135
US Information Service: 19, 20, 76/7B, 107B, 108BL, 108BR, 134B
US Navy Department, Washington: 74/5
Wells Fargo Bank History Room, San Francisco: 22T, 22B
Worden Collection/Wells Fargo Bank History Room, San Francisco: 4/5, 16/17
Picture research: Sheila A. Thomson

Published by Marshall Cavendish Publications Limited, 58 Old Compton Street, London W1V 5PA

© Marshall Cavendish Publications Limited, 1975

First Printing 1975

ISBN 0 85685 135 3

Printed in Great Britain by Severn Valley Press Limited

Introduction

Disaster is unlike anything else in human experience. It strikes quickly, it changes the lives of all it touches, and its effects are felt long after the event. And, perhaps more important, its forces are largely outside the control of the people whom it most affects.

Disasters are frequently the result of natural phenomena, themselves unaffected by the actions of mere human beings. But modern technology is capable of predicting hurricanes, tornadoes and even earthquakes. As often as not the warnings issued before such an event are ignored to a notorious degree. The real disaster, in terms of human life, almost always comes from this uniquely human failure to heed the signals. When Hurricane Camille vented its wrathful force on the Gulf Coast of the United States in the autumn of 1969, warnings were issued, asking the inhabitants of coastal towns to get to higher ground if possible. The majority of the people concerned refused to view the danger seriously. Many who stayed behind for 'hurricane parties' died in the worst ocean storm to strike the coast of the mainland USA this century.

Other disasters are built on human error, and are usually compounded by it. The 'unsinkable' *Titanic* sank because one human being after another failed to heed the danger presented by a deadly pack of icebergs in the North Atlantic; the general reluctance even to believe that such a tragedy was possible meant that there were not enough lifeboats available and most of the ones that were provided were lowered with only a few people in each. 1,503 people died on that cold night. More recently, 346 people died when a Turkish Airlines DC10 crashed outside Paris after a series of human ineptitudes resulted in the failure of an airport attendant to close a baggage door properly.

The disasters discussed here have all made an impact on our world. Either they are the worst tragedies of their kind in our century or they have had a profound effect on our 'folk' culture, like the San Francisco earthquake and Aberfan. Or they have caused the authorities responsible to think again about safety procedures which would hopefully prevent a recurrence of disaster, such as the collapse of the bridge over the Yarra River in Melbourne or the explosion at a nylon manufacturing plant in Flixborough.

They do not include disasters that result from acts of war: hence we have included the *Titanic* but not the *Lusitania*, the explosion at Flixborough but not Hiroshima. Disastrous as these are, they are created by acts of aggression rather than by natural events or human neglect.

Contents

First page *Aberfan after the slide*

Title page *Flixborough after the explosion*

4/5 *San Francisco after the earthquake*

6/7 *Quintinshill survivors after the train crash*

8/9 *Ermenonville Forest after the crash of the DC10*

May 8, 1902
Eruption of Mont Pelèe

At the turn of the century, Martinique was a pretty, prosperous French colony, nestling among the Lesser Antilles in the Caribbean. A favoured spot for summer visitors from France, the island luxuriated in tropical flowers, banana trees, sugar cane plantations and dense forests.

Its natural profusion came from the soil: rich dark volcanic matter spewed forth over centuries by the island's biggest mountain, the volcanic peak of Mont Pelèe. 4583 feet high, Pelèe dominated the landscape at the northern end of the island. Just below lay the main town of St Pierre, with 30,000 inhabitants. Further south and on the same west side of the island stood the principal port, Fort de France.

The peaceful colonial existence of the island's natives and French settlers was strangely disturbed in the early months of 1902. Although Mont Pelèe was known to be an active volcano, it had never done more than cause a few rumbles or spit out a little ash. Its main crater held a beautiful mirror-like lake, which was a favourite picnic spot for visitors from France.

Suddenly in early April, steam and great hissing noises poured from the crater. Volcanic ash began to rain down on the Indian settlements nestling in the forests of Mont Pelèe's foothills. By April 25, the activity had become so fierce and continuous that the French authorities sent a scientific commission up the mountain to investi-

Below The town of St Pierre, Martinique, nestles at the foothills of the volcanic peak of Mont Pelèe.
Right Desolation was all that remained of St Pierre after the cloud of ash and steam.

gate. A secondary crater, a little lower down than the main lake, was rapidly filling with water. Previously, it had been a dry hollow called the *Etang Sec*, or 'dry pool'. A new cinder cone, a product of volcanic activity, was pushing its way up through the boiling water and rising steam.

The commission seems to have approached this phenomenon with great scientific interest, but with little apprehension for people's safety. The island's main newspaper, *Les Colonies*, published the scientific finding: there was no reason to be afraid. In various editorial comments, the paper mocked those citizens who were beginning to express fears.

Nothing short of folly could have induced people to ignore nature's warnings. Life on Martinique became more unendurable day by day. A hideous odour of sulphur filled the air towards the end of April. The wife of the American consul, Mrs Prentiss, recorded, 'The smell of it is so strong that horses on the street stop and snort, and some of them drop in their harness and die of suffocation. Many of the people are obliged to wear wet handkerchiefs to protect them from the strong fumes of sulphur'.

A continuous pall of grey ash hung over the north end of the island. Trees looked as if a light snowstorm had descended; the Jardin des Plantes, where rare tropical blooms were reared for dispatch to the famous hothouse garden in Paris, was smothered in a film of silver: palms, ravenalas, mangoes, rubber trees, cacti and hibiscus were all drained of colour. Soon, birds dropped out of the sky, asphyxiated by ash and sulphur. By May 3, many businessmen in St Pierre put up their shutters, as prudent individuals moved bag and baggage to the southern part of the island.

Yet *Les Colonies* maintained its air of quiet mockery at the despondency. It prattled about possible excursions to see the wonder of nature at work. A setback occurred on May 5 when a giant boil of mud spewed out of Pelèe's crater and down the Rivière Blanche. It completely smothered the Guerin factory lying directly in its path, killing 30 employees inside. Now citizens began to flee in greater number. Yet on May 7, *Les Colonies* ran an interview with a distinguished French professor, M. Landes, in which he declared with confidence that Mont Pelèe presented 'no more danger to the inhabitants of St Pierre than does Vesuvius to those of Naples'. By modern safety standards this was hardly a great recommendation. The Italian volcano Vesuvius is chiefly famous for the great eruption of AD 79 that wiped out the towns of Pompeii, Stabiae and Herculaneum. It has seldom remained silent in its long history. In the 50 years between 1850 and 1900 it had erupted five times. Still, many citizens chose to ignore the evidence. That same day, May 7, the newspaper reported on the mass exodus and added, 'We confess we cannot understand this panic. Where could one be better off than at St Pierre?' While 300 citizens a day left, the town's population grew with the intake of refugees from the villages on Pelèe's slopes. The

May 7 newspaper carried a small footnote, 'Our offices being closed tomorrow, the next issue will appear on Friday.'

There never was another issue. At 4am on Thursday, May 8, a giant thunderstorm broke over Fort de France, lighting up the whole west coast of Martinique. At 7.30am the skies cleared, and from the port a high column of black smoke could be seen billowing up from Mont Pelèe. The cloud glistened with millions of shiny particles described by one eye witness as a 'whole cloud surface fairly scintillating with dancing lights'. Rumblings, explosive noises and then loud detonations filled the air for at least an hour.

The inhabitants of Fort de France gathered on the quayside to watch the strange scene taking place 14 miles to the north. At 8.50, a gigantic wave receded from the shores of the port and then flooded back to the brink at a height increased by at least two feet. At 9.18 a staggering flash of lightning shaped like a lightbulb filament or balloon looped across the northeast sky. The black cloud grew bigger and bigger, mushrooming, billowing, shooting out sparks that could be seen miles away. Lightning flashes and thunder filled the air. Orange serpents, S-shaped streaks of electrical discharges, produced spectacular effects against the black rolling mass.

This violent activity continued into the afternoon, culminating in a terrific storm. An eye witness in Fort de France recorded the final outburst. 'The steam cloud, with a velocity of 20mph came overhead, grey and tongue-shaped. It spread across the vault, producing darkness, when it reached the zenith, pebbles fell about the size of a chestnut, cold, and these became a rattling hail diminishing to the size of peas. Then fine grey ash followed. . . .'

From a ship just outside St Pierre itself, the

Above The cloud of ash and steam hailed down stones the size of chestnuts on the city; hot grey ash set fire to wooden structures. Billowing clouds of steam crawled through the streets, and soon the whole of St Pierre was engulfed in flame and rubble.

Right The tower of Pelèe, made of thick lava, pushed upwards through the growing dome.

Below right A view of the volcanic storm clouds that billowed out of Pelèe's summit during the volcanic eruption. Thunder, flashing sparks and trails of curved lightning filled the air for miles around.

eruption of Pelèe looked as if the mountain had blown to pieces. A cloud of fire and mud rolled down over the town, over the sea, over the ships. A great tidal wave crashed the vessels on to the shore, where they lay listing and smouldering, their top decks on fire.

St Pierre was totally engulfed in that billowing black cloud. All 30,000-odd people within its limits, many attending Ascension Day church services, were smothered and burned to death. The extraordinary feature of Pelèe's eruption was that very little lava-flow caused damage. People were killed by a blistering mixture of 1500°F steam and noxious gases. Just one citizen lived to tell the tale—a 28-year-old native shoemaker called Leon Comprère-Leandre.

'I was seated on a doorstep of my house which was in the southeast part of the city . . . all of a sudden I felt a terrible wind blowing, the earth began to tremble, and the sky suddenly became dark.' Leon ran inside, where he was joined by several other people off the street seeking shelter. They all lay down, and one by one succumbed to the heat and lack of oxygen. Leon himself lay in agony on his bed, his throat and lungs bursting with pain, waiting to die. 'My sense returned to me in perhaps an hour, my legs bleeding and covered in burns, I ran to Fonds-Saint-Denis, six kilometres from St Pierre. I heard no human cries . . . the entire city was aflame.'

Meanwhile at Fort de France, a ship was being prepared to sail north round the point that separated it from St Pierre. No news had come from the town, and the port people were anxious. The Vicar General of Fort de France, M. Parel, boarded the vessel and set sail for St Pierre. He made a historic record of the terrible scene that awaited the sea-borne party.

All the ships in the harbour were burning fiercely. The whole town was a mass of fire. 'No living soul', wrote M. Parel, 'appears in this desert of desolation, encompassed by appalling silence.' Mount Pelèe in the background was covered with a thick film of white ash, rising like an alpine peak above the ruins below. A region of eight to nine square miles was completely destroyed, and all the vegetation was killed for miles around. Three towns, St Pierre, Basse Pointe and Prêcheur, were obliterated by the black steam. M. Parel concluded, '. . . the city [of St Pierre] was laid to smouldering ruins, coated with ash-paste, and looking as if it were built of adobe plaster. What had before been the vivid colouring of houses of the tropics was now ashen grey.'

Yet worse disaster followed. On May 20 an earthquake shook the island, flattening the little that remained among the cinders of St Pierre and causing further damage to Fort de France. The editor of the newspaper, *Les Colonies*, had died in the first eruption; otherwise, he no doubt would have had something to say about the mass exodus that now took place. Thousands fled to the nearby islands of St Lucia, Guadeloupe and Trinidad or went further afield to new lives in France and the USA. As Vicar General M. Parel put it, 'It is no

Right *The structure of a volcano. Fissures in the earth's crust allow molten rock and gases to erupt and a cone of solidified lava builds up.*
Below *Like the inhabitants of Martinique, the people of Pompeii ignored warnings and were caught by the eruption of Mt Vesuvius in AD79. Many bodies have been found perfectly preserved in ash where they fell in streets and homes.*
Bottom *Vesuvius last erupted in 1944, spewing its lava into the Bay of Naples below.*

longer the exodus of the north to the south, but of all Martinique to foreign lands . . . I can but follow the example of Father Mary and of his fellow priests of the northern parishes. I shall be the last to leave Martinique.'

Out of the upheaval of Mont Pelèe, a giant obelisk rose up above the ash-filled valley. 'Spines' of this sort are created by extra-thick lava that pushes up through the growing dome in a straight pile instead of falling down the slope in a runny mass. This 'Tower of Pelèe' was a spectacular example of the phenomenon. At its maximum it rose 2000 feet high. Its destruction occurred in gradual stages. Explosions round its base as early as July 1903 caused it to crack and collapse. All the time, the volcano continued to roar and rumble, filling the sky with glowing colour and sparkling particles.

Several features of the Pelèe volcanic eruption make it unique among natural disasters. It caused a greater disturbance in the earth's magnetic field than any previously recorded. Sound waves from the explosions reached as far as 1000 miles away. The electric illumination of the sky and the giant serpents of lightning were extraordinary manifestations of the volcano's disturbance. The shock waves and earth tremors recorded reached almost to Krakatoa proportions—the great volcano in the straits of Sunda between Sumatra and Java had erupted in 1883, causing a mighty flood that killed 40,000 people on the Javanese coast. It was the greatest explosion in world history, and when it had ended, Krakatoa had disappeared. The explosions of Krakatoa were heard 2200 miles away. Spectacular sunsets lit up the skies all over the world for a year afterwards. Mont Pelèe provided the same brilliant red skies, and afterglows were reported off Venezuela, the coast of California, in Honolulu and in Europe from Italy to England. The steam and ash from Pelèe hurled up four to six miles into the sky. Krakatoa had spewed forth volcanic matter to a height of 50 miles.

That French expert, M. Landes, had mentioned Vesuvius as a reassuring comparison. What a strange prophecy. Just as the citizens of Pompeii were buried where they stood in a massive lava flow, so too St Pierre was wiped out in a matter of seconds. The curious difference was the absence of lava. Destruction was caused by superheated steam travelling at a speed of one and a half to three miles per minute as it left the summit.

The tragedy of Pelèe is the almost total absence of preparation by the citizens of St Pierre. Ignoring all signs, they lived from day to day in a state of suspended judgement. It is perhaps the strangest and most dangerous of human reactions to impending disaster, and one that is extremely difficult to overcome.

Above right *Europe's highest volcano is Mount Etna in Sicily. Over 10,000 feet high, it is constantly active.*
Below right *Main areas of volcanic activity.*

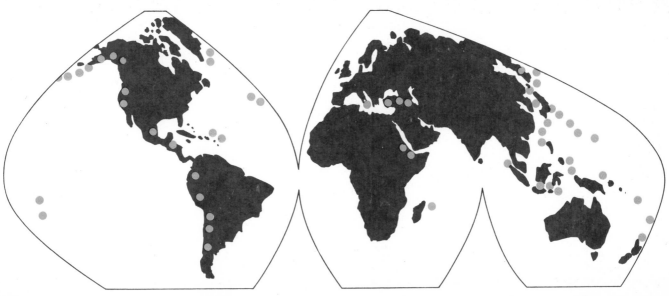

April 18, 1906
San Francisco
Earthquake

The San Francisco earthquake brought the end of an era to the Californian city, an era of adventurousness, constant change and lawlessness. The city had grown on the profits of the gold rush in an uncontrolled sprawl. Within its boundaries lay the rich stone-built mansions of prominent families who had made fortunes in the new prosperity and lived as elegantly as Parisians. Nearby were wide areas of wooden, rickety houses where the poorer folk lived shoulder-to-shoulder with crime and corruption. There was the 'Barbary Coast'—a famous strip of saloons, dance-halls, gambling houses and brothels, decked out in red and plush magnificence, where no man's purse was safe and where unfortunates might disappear without trace on a dark night.

The very location of the city demonstrates its precarious existence—and its tenacity. It lies between two major earthquake faultlines, the cause of frequent tremors and rumblings. The San Andreas fault runs from Cape Mendocino, to the north of San Francisco Bay, right down to the Colorado Desert, by-passing most of the city itself, but sidling under the harbour and the Golden Gate Bridge. It is 600 miles long and goes into the middle of the earth approximately 700 miles. At its centre lies a core of metal, mainly iron, surrounded by a crust of hot plastic matter and covered by a layer of solid rock. If the pressure on

the fault is shifted even a fractional amount, the underlying material becomes more plastic and malleable and moves about, finding another way to settle. This activity results in an earthquake.

San Francisco had experienced so many disasters in its short, dramatic history that there was no panic when the major catastrophe of 1906 took place, but a remarkable degree of courage and adaptability. The city's population in 1848 was 800. Then a builder found huge nuggets of gold at the famous Sutter's Mill site (the name now given to a major downtown street) and a mass influx of money-hungry Easterners swelled the city to 40,000 by 1860, only 12 years later.

The crowds brought problems, the worst being fire. In '49 a great blaze broke out among the lean-to houses and wooden huts. But in four short months, a million dollars' worth of damage was replaced. In 1850, four city-wide blazes occurred and rumours of gangs of 'fire-raisers' or 'hoodlums' spread. More fires followed in '53 and '54. If that danger were not enough, pronounced earth tremors were felt in '57, '65 and '90, caused by the San Andreas fault, while the Hayward fault, to the east and inland, caused another in 1868 which was felt just as clearly as the rest.

Around the turn of the century, civic pride set in and many public officials began to take firm steps to clean up the city and make it the jewel of

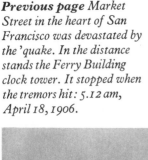

Previous page Market Street in the heart of San Francisco was devastated by the 'quake. In the distance stands the Ferry Building clock tower. It stopped when the tremors hit: 5.12 am, April 18, 1906.

the West Coast. By 1906 the population stood at about 450,000. Civic amenities had improved: elegant parks, fine hotels, expensive shops and the famous cable-car system transformed San Francisco into a sophisticated metropolis—on the surface. Below, however, there were still ruinous activities. Fire Chief Danny Sullivan warned city officials repeatedly that not enough measures had been taken to protect the city from really serious fire. Worse still, the main water-supply pipes into the city had been laid on a line directly across the known path of the San Andreas fault. The dramatic increase in the population and business enterprises in the city had led to the practice of 'filling' land around the bay to create more space for housing and warehouses. By the end of 1853 there were 30 blocks of 'made' land where buildings stood, and by 1906 that area was vastly increased. People knew it was dangerous, for as early as 1902 and 1903, there had been reports of its gradual tendency to sink. But San Francisco was convinced that her prosperity could only go on from strength to strength and that her citizens were clever and adventurous enough to face anything the future could bring.

Fortune put them to a hard test. On the evening of Tuesday April 17, 1906, the city was more than usually crowded. The Metropolitan Opera of New York was in town, and the great Caruso himself was giving the opening night performance of *Carmen*. All the smart downtown hotels were full, like the Palace, famous for its beautiful glass-domed centre courtyard into which the clientele could drive in state in their horse-drawn carriages.

After a night of music, drinking, dancing, San Francisco went to bed. At exactly 5 hours, 12 minutes and 38 seconds on the morning of April 18, the whole city woke up. For what must have been the longest minute in their lives, the citizens were subjected to a monumental rocking and shaking throughout their entire world. A deafeningly deep rumble and roar filled the air. People were hurled out of bed; furniture rocked about; china, glass and silver came crashing down in great smashed heaps. Chimneys fell, clocks stopped, windows fell to the ground below. One of the official earthquake commissioners later reported lying in bed and watching fascinated as a large oak wardrobe in the middle of his room swung first to the west, then to the north, then to the east, and finally fell directly to the south, splintering into pieces, such was the force of the motion. More horrendous, another man lay in his lodging house watching the plaster fall off the ceiling. Then a child's foot appeared. As the building swayed and compressed with the force of the tremor, the hole closed over, the child's foot broke off, and with no more thought, the

Above *Tramlines lying
north to south along the
main lines of force of the
earthquake were buckled
and thrown into the air as
arches.*

dazed sleeper hurled himself through an open window before the whole structure collapsed.

In that one minute, horizontal waves of energy buckled and twisted the earth, making great gashes in its surface and cracking walls like eggshells. The first shock lasted 30 seconds; then there was a deathly ten seconds of peace before a second, more intense tremor went on for a further 25.

Luck favoured San Francisco, for if the earthquake had occurred in the middle of the day, there would have been a much greater loss of life. Most people were protected inside houses. In all earthquakes, the greatest danger is from falling masonry, flying glass and earth upheaval.

An editor of the leading newspaper, the San Francisco *Examiner*, was among the small proportion caught in the open air. He had just left his office with some colleagues after finishing the morning edition. As they stood chatting on a street corner, the earth began to sway beneath their feet. They were thrown flat on their faces, and as they looked up in amazement, they saw whole buildings dance. Clouds of dust rose on all sides and storms of glass and brick rained to the ground. Everywhere, people were crawling about on all fours like insects. The tracks of the trolley buses were lifted into the air, the thicknesses of metal coiled about like spaghetti loops and flash-

ed blue sparks as the current short-circuited. A smell of gas began to seep into the air. The main force of the earthquake was from north to south through the city: gas mains in streets lying east to west were broken and drawn apart, while those north to south were crushed and telescoped together or raised above the ground in arches, like the tram lines.

In Valencia Street, the water pipes broke as the force of the earthquake made the ground sink six feet on either side of the road. The Valencia Street Hotel simply slouched down and people in rooms on the fourth floor walked out through their windows on to the street.

The temperamental Señor Caruso in the Palace Hotel was so shocked that his first thought was to test his voice to make sure he hadn't lost it through fright. He flung his window open wide and it is said that he thought he sang the finest notes of his life in the following seconds. He picked up his valise and pushed his way through the jumble of screaming people running like ants all over the hotel. He got to the street, where he sat for a while on his suitcase. Then he somehow made his way up the hill to the Saint Francis Hotel, where everyone pampered him, trying to soothe his shattered nerves. He could be heard muttering, ''ell of a place, 'ell of a place, I never come back.' He never did: he got back to New

York six days later and refused to discuss the experience any further.

But few native San Franciscans thought of running away. Some who lived on the outskirts, mainly to the north where the 'quake was not so severe, actually formed sightseeing parties to come and gaze at the spectacle on the south side of the city—the ruined downtown shopping and financial district, and beyond that, below Market Street, the Mission area, where poorer housing was totally obliterated. In the downtown area, whole blocks of buildings were flattened. One landmark still stood out, the Ferry Building with its clock tower. The timepiece had stopped at the exact moment that the earthquake took place.

The pride of San Francisco, the newly-built City Hall, was completely destroyed. This caused quite an uproar, for the authorities had been told that no effort would be spared in materials and labour to make the structure tremor-proof and sound. Now only the dome and some supporting pillars remained, accusatory evidence of corner-cutting materials and shoddy work.

But the Post Office miraculously stood firm, more or less intact. Built of steel and granite, it rested on piles driven a considerable depth into the earth. Within a few yards of its west corner, the streets were deformed into great waves, showing the degree of pressures the structure had resisted. Fissures three feet wide appeared in the ground and arches lifted the pavements, but only the mosaics in the building's interior corridors fell down.

No one ever knew exactly how many people had died in the earthquake itself. Possibly a few hundred lives were lost as a direct result of buildings collapsing or from injuries sustained at the time.

Worse danger was still to come—San Francisco's old enemy, fire, began to break out in localized spots all over the city within ten minutes after the tremor. Yet people seemed oblivious to the oncoming danger. Most were so relieved to have survived the earthquake that they began piecing together their lives by cooking a hearty breakfast in the street, right in front of their collapsed homes. The famous 'ham and eggs' fire was started by a housewife on Van Ness Avenue. Without thought as to the possibility of broken mains, she lit a match, causing an explosion and subsequent fire that levelled several blocks of the city. Lawlessness broke out—people raided shops, seizing food, clothing, anything they could lay their hands on. For some people breakfast that day brought new experiences of delicatessen savouries and canned luxuries far beyond their usual food budgets.

While the citizens milled around in a daze,

Above *A scandal revealed: San Francisco's City Hall was newly built to be earthquake-proof. Only the dome survived, clear evidence of shoddy materials.*

EXTRA THE DAILY NEWS EXTRA

VOl, 7. NO. 25. FOURTH YEAR.   SAN FRANCISCO, WEDNESDAY EVENING, APRIL 18, 1906   INDEPENDENT. 25c MONTH; 1 COPY.

HUNDREDS DEAD!

Fire Follows Earthquake, Laying Downtown Section in Ruins--City Seems Doomed For Lack of Water

KNOWN DEAD AT MECHANICS' PAVILION

Max Fenner, policeman, killed

At 126 Langton, 4 killed; Billy Sheehan, policeman, rescued 3 people.

Many injured at 117 6th st., Hotel Phillips.

San Francisco was practically demolished and totally paralyzed by the earthquake, which commenced at 5:1... m to...

Francisco Bay.

A building collapsed at Steiner and Haight sts. No report of loss of life.

Along Market st. from 5th toward Castro, the sidewalk... erally strewn with wreckage. In ...walks have collapsed ...

Above Scare headlines on The Daily News *did little to alleviate the fears of the population, but the Mayor's proclamation* **below right** *helped to calm the situation.*

attempting to help themselves, they must have thought that someone somewhere would soon take charge of the fires, and then everything would be all right. But Fire Chief Sullivan was dead, killed by a falling chimney, and his deputy Dougherty took charge. Soon, all Sullivan's warnings about the inadequacy of the city's fire-fighting resources would be proven in a catastrophic lesson. In the first hour or so after the 'quake, 52 fires were reported to the fire department, but the force only had 38 horse-drawn fire engines. The teams set out bravely amid the wreck of the city, but when they got near the fires and tried connecting their hoses to the street hydrants, they realized the terrible truth: San Francisco was without water. The whole city's supply had been cut off by the earthquake. Sullivan had advocated developing a system of using sea-water, envisaging this situation, but as salt corrodes hose pipes and fitments, the plan had seemed unrealistic. Now reality stared the firemen in the face. The whole city might go up in flames and there was nothing they could do about it.

They tried nobly. In some places, tanks fed by artesian wells yielded small supplies of water. Then the fire brigade tried dynamiting buildings in the path of the blaze to check its progress. But they had little experience in how to use the charges and created terror with the severity of their explosions. Besides, using too much explosive meant that buildings blew apart, leaving interior woodwork exposed to the oncoming flames, rather than collapsing the houses into a heap of brick.

San Francisco's officials rose to the challenge of the occasion with bravery and decisiveness. Mayor Eugene Schmitz immediately summoned a Relief Committee comprising 50 of San Francisco's leading citizens. Throughout the day they worked tirelessly, often forced to move by the

ever-encroaching flames—from house to house across the city. Federal troops were quickly summoned by Brigadier-General Funston from nearby Fort Mason. Fifteen hundred soldiers helped firemen in their struggle against the blaze and also began to patrol the streets in an effort to control the rampant looting. Mayor Schmitz's first proclamation of the day was exactly what the situation required.

PROCLAMATION BY THE MAYOR

The Federal Troops, the members of the Regular Police Force and all Special Police Officers have been authorized by me to KILL any and all persons found engaged in Looting or in the Commission of Any Other Crime.

I have directed all the Gas and Electric Lighting Co.'s not to turn on Gas or Electricity until I order them to do so. You may therefore expect the city to remain in darkness for an indefinite time.

I request all citizens to remain at home from darkness until daylight every night until order is restored.

I WARN all Citizens of the danger of fire from Damaged or Destroyed Chimneys, Broken or Leaking Gas Pipes or Fixtures, or any like cause.

E. E. SCHMITZ, Mayor

Dated, April 18, 1906.

ALTVATER PRINT, MISSION AND 22D STS.

The chief merit of Schmitz's proclamations was that they helped to keep people informed about what was happening in the city. A frightening aspect of disaster is that people rapidly become bewildered and full of panic. They lose relatives and friends and have no knowledge about what might happen to them. Schmitz realized the danger of widespread loss of morale.

By mid-day the fire had become more or less uncontrollable. Schmitz was forced to declare a conflagration. Still, there was little panic. People began to bundle their belongings together and to proceed as best they could to fire-free areas. Around the Ferry Building, hordes of people attempted to get across the bay to Oakland where tremors had been felt but which had sustained little damage. The Navy took charge of the ferry and kept it going all through the afternoon of the 18th and the following night. That 50,000 got across to safety was a miracle, because the area around the Ferry Building, on the southeast side of the city, was the worst affected both by the earthquake and the fire. Wharves and warehouses were ablaze, and only non-stop effort kept the access to the ferry itself from succumbing to the flames.

Further aid for the stranded and homeless soon came from outside San Francisco. The one serviceable telegraph wire had been reserved immediately for official use, so that within a few hours, the outside world knew of the disaster overtaking the entire city. The National Guard, 600 cadets from the University of California, and two fire boats, *Active* and *Leslie*, were dispatched, these last on the orders of President Theodore Roosevelt, to relieve the city. A Red Cross ship, *Prebble*, arrived with medical supplies. The injured were housed at first in the Mechanic's Pavilion, but this too was threatened by fire and everyone had to be evacuated again.

One newspaper, the *Daily News*, managed to appear on the historic day of the earthquake, though its coverage of the event did considerably less than the Mayor's proclamations to calm fears.

For days afterwards, the *Daily News* carried small ads, free of cost, in which citizens could advertize for the whereabouts of relatives lost in the general disorder that the fire caused.

The fire took its toll with no regard to status. Chinatown, a colourful district of restaurants, bars, laundries, bakeries, brothels and drug dens was completely wiped out. Its destruction ended rumours that the area was riddled with miles of underground corridors where white-slavers and drug-pushers plied their trades. When the ashes cooled, only tiny basement rooms were found

Below *Survivors remained cheerful in temporary camps.*
Bottom *Major earthquake areas of the world. Scientists are currently discovering methods of predicting the occurrence of earthquakes, both location and strength, more accurately.*

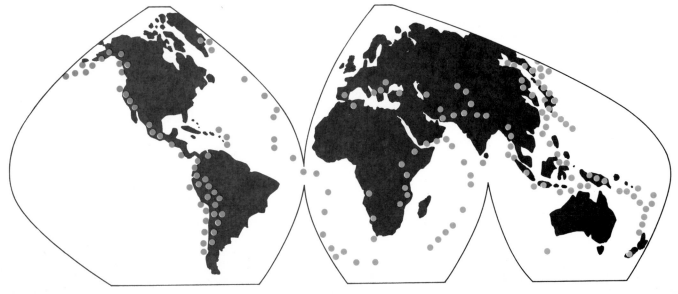

beneath the rubble of the quarter.

At the other end of town, many of the richest families in San Francisco saw their entire fortunes go up in smoke. The fire-fighting forces tried lighting back-fires to run towards the blaze, so that when the two walls of fire met, the sheets of flame would die out. To do this and to create blank areas in the path of the fire, many fine mansions, notably on Van Ness Avenue on the west side of the city, were laid waste. Some braver men stood and watched their established homes, full of antiques, rare china, paintings and books, vanish before their eyes. Others turned and drove away with their families, unable to watch their hard-earned comforts disappear in minutes.

Some municipal buildings were saved from destruction by the determined efforts of officials unwilling to allow dynamite or fire to overtake them. The new Mint Building luckily had its own water supply in tanks on the roof, so teams of volunteers extinguished the fire there and continued working in its defence as the day progressed. Postmaster Arthur Fish conducted a similar exercise to protect the Post Office Building. Miraculously eight clerks emerged unscathed from the rubble inside the building three days later.

Some citizens showed remarkable optimism in the face of disaster. There was an unprecedented run on wedding licences that day, rising to seven an hour at the worst moments. An enterprising clerk from the City Hall had saved a book of licence blanks.

A surprisingly large number of people showed no desire to leave San Francisco. They gathered in the parks and open areas on the northwest corner of the city in Golden Gate Park and the Presidio. Soon, supplies of tents came in by order of William Taft, the Secretary for War, and enormous relief encampments of canvas and wood began to spring up in the green spaces. Some of these were still there two years later, though rebuilding and rehousing started at a generally fast rate.

The fire continued to rage uncontrolled Thursday and Friday, but a light rain on Saturday helped at last to put it out. In any case, by then there was little left for the fire to feed on.

On Sunday Mayor Schmitz published another Proclamation:

'The fire is now under control and all danger is passed. The only fear is that other fires may start should people build fires in their stoves, and I therefore want all citizens not to build fires in their stoves until the chimneys have been inspected and repaired properly . . . I congratulate the citizens of San Francisco upon the fortitude they have displayed and urge upon them the necessity of aiding the authorities in the work of relieving the destitute and the suffering.'

Destitution and suffering was all around. Although only a few hundred lost their lives (estimates vary from 400 to 1000), the devastation was immense. A total area of four square miles of the city centre was completely burnt out, and 28,188 houses were destroyed by the earthquake and the ensuing fire. The whole area that felt the vibrations of the earthquake was much greater—covering 372,700 square miles. In outlying areas the shock waves were read by machines, but from Oregon to Los Angeles, a distance of 730 miles, people could feel the effects with their own unaided senses.

Efforts to recover were made immediately. As soon as railway track was operational, the independent railway companies provided free transport for those who had homes in other states. On the second day after the disaster, 70 passengers per minute were moved in trains totalling ten miles in length. South Pacific Railroad took out 300,000 passengers and brought in emergency supplies, food and medical materials, all free of charge. Soon, all over the city, soup kitchens were set up by the Relief Committee, manned by citizens who had not suffered in the disaster. And in the camps the pioneering spirit soon reasserted itself, and dingy old photographs reveal straight-eyed craggy-featured individuals sitting upright in front of canvas walls bearing inscriptions like 'Ring the Bell for Landlady. Furnished rooms with running water, steam heating and ELEVATOR.'

Within two weeks, electricity supplies were in order again and street cars began to operate on streets where the road surface permitted. Market Street, the main downtown thoroughfare, was blocked by rubble, and the working parties there established an unofficial ruling that any able-bodied man who passed by had to dig for 20 minutes. The road was cleared in half a day.

The prevailing attitude of self-help and co-operation was a notable feature of the recovery process. The first big question in everyone's mind concerned insurance policies. Most firms paid up without hesitation or at least with only a short delay, and helped to get the city on its feet again. A relief fund was set up and soon money was pouring in from all over the world. $185,244,198 was received, together with $2,500,000 from an official Government contribution.

There was no question of leaving San Francisco as a ruin, in spite of the continuing threat of earthquakes. Fifty-two small tremors shook the region in the two days after the disaster, and minor shudders are experienced to this day. On March 22, 1957, a further 'quake was experienced but nowhere near the severity of 1906, which registered 8.25 on the Richter Scale. San Francisco rebuilt, with some well-learned lessons. Buildings made with steel reinforcement stand up better to tremors than wood, brick or pure stone. Land made by filling up spaces of open water is less dangerous on the whole than land made by depositing a thin rigid layer of fill on tracts of marshland (which was the construction in the Mission area). Most important, a proper fire-fighting agency is essential in a city where such calamity is a distinct possibility.

April 14, 1912
Sinking of the Titanic

The *Titanic* was launched on May 31, 1911 amidst a great fanfare. The enormous liner was the ultimate in sea-going luxury, displacing 66,000 tons, 104 feet high, 882·5 feet long, with two sets of 4-cylinder reciprocating engines producing 50,000 registered horsepower and a cruising speed of 24 to 25 knots. She could carry 3000 people in her luxuriously appointed three-class cabins. Her most publicized feature was her special construction, for she was divided into 16 separate watertight compartments. Her owners, the White Star Line, claimed that this made her virtually unsinkable.

Among her star attractions were expensive period furnishings, an exotically-decorated Turkish bath and the finest cuisine that money could buy. Not surprisingly, her maiden voyage prompted first-class bookings from the highest strata of society: countesses, lords, millionaires and industrial magnates made up a passenger list worth $250 million. Such an auspicious start to the *Titanic*'s career merited the presence on board of the President of the White Star Line himself, Bruce Ismay.

On April 10, 1912, the *Titanic* glided out of Southampton harbour bound for New York. The first few days of the voyage realized all the dreams of both owners and passengers: service was immaculate, dining and wining a positive delight, and the *beau monde* of Europe and America renewed old acquaintances and struck up new ones in an atmosphere of privileged security. Even their maids, valets and nannies received special attention from the seemingly endless army of ship's servants and had their own lounge on the 'C' deck.

Inflated self-confidence proved to be the *Titanic*'s disastrous end. This story of folly began on Sunday, April 14. The wireless operator, John Phillips, was busily sending out passengers' messages to Cape Race—radio was then still a novelty and the smart set made full use of it to let friends and relatives know their anticipated arrival time. In between the flood of personal cables, Phillips kept getting odd signals from other ships on the main transatlantic route ahead, from the *Caronia*, the *Baltic* and the *Californian*. There seemed to be large ice packs moving unusually far south from the chilly waters of the Arctic circle. About noon the *Baltic* tapped out: 'Have had moderate variable winds and clear fine weather since leaving. Greek steamer *Athenai* reports passing icebergs and large quantities of field ice today in Latitude 41·51° north, Longitude 49·52° west . . .'

In the first of a series of stupidities, this message somehow got into the hands of President Bruce Ismay, whose position on the liner alternated between *ex officio* Commodore and star guest, depending on the mood of the moment. Despite the significance of its contents, the message was shown to various lady passengers during the afternoon, but it did not get to the chartroom, where some sense might have been made of it, until 7.15pm. Meanwhile the *Titanic* proceeded on an unchanged course.

At about the same time, the temperature around the ship began to drop perceptibly from 43°F, to freezing point at about 10pm. Still no one in authority took the slightest notice. The radio officer could have taken action on a message intercepted around 7.30, from the *Californian* to the *Antillian*, again reporting three large icebergs. At 9.40, a third message was received by the *Titanic* from the *Mesaba*: 'Much heavy pack ice and a great number of large icebergs'. These two messages were never delivered to the bridge.

A blind disregard of all warning signs seemed to be leading the great liner into calamity. Only human fallibility can explain what happened when at 11pm the *Californian* directly contacted the *Titanic* to announce that it was totally hemmed in by ice and had stopped engines. John Phillips, by this time worn out with the day's work, could contain his irritation no longer. 'Shut up, shut up, I am busy!' he snapped back. His fatigue was evident to his right-hand man, second operator Bride, who came on duty at midnight, instead of at 2am, to relieve him.

The immediacy of the danger was beginning to dawn on Captain Edward Smith. By now the coldness of the air had prompted him to post six look-outs to watch for ice, but the passengers went to bed between 10 and 11pm unaware of any problem. Simultaneously, the *Titanic* drew so close that the ice-bound *Californian* could actually see her lights in the distance.

At 11.40, the mighty ship experienced a staggering collision with a giant iceberg. The look-outs had seen it, but the *Titanic* was upon the ice before the signal to reverse engines could have any effect. An enormous hole was ripped along one-third the length of the ship. Almost instantly the engine rooms began to fill with water.

Most people, including Bruce Ismay, only felt a 'slight judder', so massive was the bulk of the liner. But Ismay was experienced enough to sense that something untoward had taken place, so he got up and went to the bridge.

Meanwhile 3rd officer Charles Groves on the *Californian* saw the lights of the big ship go out,

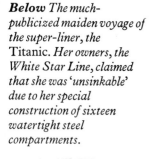

Below *The much-publicized maiden voyage of the super-liner, the* Titanic. *Her owners, the White Star Line, claimed that she was 'unsinkable' due to her special construction of sixteen watertight steel compartments.*

but thought they had been turned off on purpose to give the hint to the few remaining wide-awake passengers. He could not know that the *Titanic* had swung sharply to port.

Those already in bed thought the whole incident was a huge joke. In one cabin, a man from Philadelphia had left his port-hole open and chunks of ice fell in on his bed as the iceberg slithered by. Other late-night drinkers in the first-class bar jumped from their seats to rush out and admire the floating hulks in the ocean, but soon retired to the coziness again and went on playing cards.

Down on the third-class deck, the humbler passengers were playing 'iceballs' and tripping back to their cabins with strange souvenirs: little cold lumps that soon melted in the warmth of the *Titanic*'s cabins.

Captain Smith knew the situation was serious. At 11.50 he ordered the radio room to send out immediate calls for help. Phillips, still there, tapped out the international 'CQD' and gave the ship's position, about 1500 miles from New York. Then Bride, just appearing to take over duty and hearing the momentous news, suggested they try the new 'SOS' signal. The *Titanic* made history as the first vessel in distress to use the new code.

A North German Lloyd steamer, the *Frankfurt*, answered first, followed by the Cunard Line *Carpathia*, some 58 miles away, and the Canadian Pacific vessel, called the *Mount Temple*.

Now the passengers began to realize something was wrong. The engines had stopped. The ship began to list frighteningly as the water relentlessly filled up room after room in the lower decks. Some of the third-class 'steerage' passengers, tucked away on the lower decks, awoke to find the floor of their cabins already awash.

Captain Smith knew the *Titanic* would sink. The water had risen 14 feet above the keel within the first ten minutes. The 'unsinkable' ship could keep afloat if any two of her 16 watertight compartments were flooded, even with three or four of her first five submerged. But the gash in her side meant that all five were filling rapidly. Even with automatic blocking mechanisms shutting off one compartment from another, the water would rise from the fifth up the stairways and through windows into the sixth, the seventh, the fifteenth in an unstoppable surge. At 12.05, the Captain ordered the lifeboats to be launched and in true-Brit old-world fashion, the word went out: 'Women and children first.'

Many stewards had to summon passengers still peacefully sleeping and get them up to the deck. There had been no lifeboat drill, and no practice at tying on life jackets, so there was bewilderment about where to go and what to do. Only the top-ranking officers and Bruce Ismay himself knew the awful truth about the lifeboat situation. There

Publicity pictures from London newspapers of the day.
Left *The ship's captain, E. J. Smith Cmdr, RNR.*
Top right *The Parisian cafe, in the style of a luxury hotel.*
Bottom right *For keep-fit fans, the latest equipment in a floating gymnasium.*

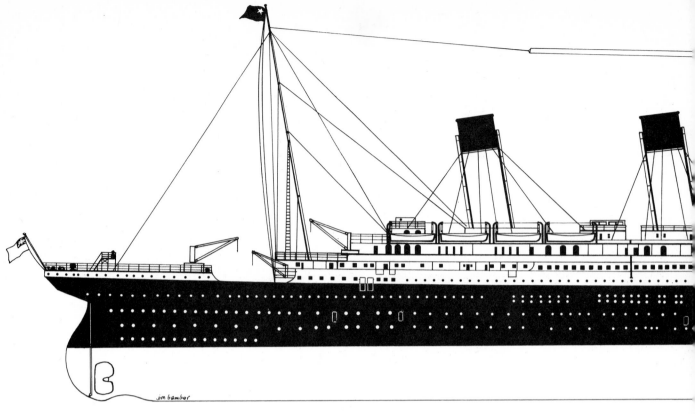

jim bomber

were only enough to take off just over half the passengers. The White Star Line had voluntarily exceeded the current legal requirements in this respect. Ship's regulations, worked out on a hopelessly inappropriate basis, called for the *Titanic* to carry boats for a maximum capacity of 962 people, whereas those supplied could carry 1178. On board that night were 2201 people, 1316 of whom were passengers. A third of those were female.

There was no raging storm, no fire and no mass panic, yet over half the people aboard the 'safest liner in the world' would be dead before the night was done.

Among the first-class passengers, husbands and fathers acted with admirable bravery, forcing their weeping wives and children to get into the lifeboats as the crew prepared them. Many ladies ran back to their cabins, seemingly oblivious of the urgency of the situation, to rescue fur coats, jewellery or other favoured trinkets. They presented an extraordinary picture, standing on the deck in lavish evening gowns, silken nightdresses and feathered hats.

Fifth officer Harold Lowe was busily ordering many of the women into Lifeboat Fourteen when Bruce Ismay approached, officiously telling everyone to hurry along and get off fast. Lowe lost his temper, and in spite of Ismay's high office, bellowed at him words to the effect 'If you'll get the hell out of the way, I'll be able to do something! You want me to lower away quickly? You'll have me drown the lot of them!' Other crew members looked shocked: Lowe would have had it when they all got to New York. But Ismay turned away without protest. He knew the true likelihood of survival. Lifeboat Fourteen got off with 55 people —one of the fuller boats. There were damning

scenes of selfishness among others escaping the now rapidly sinking ship. Number One was lowered with only 12 people, when its capacity was 40. Sir Cosmo and Lady Duff Gordon, her secretary, two Americans, six stokers and one of the ice look-out men, Symons, made up the load. Number Six went down at 12.55, Number Three at 1am, Number Eight at 1.10am. Number Five shoved off with 40 people, when it could have held 65.

The figures prove conclusively that the first-class passengers were looked after in preference to the lower classes. Only four of the first-class women died, three by choice, when they refused to be separated from their husbands. One of these was Mrs Isador Straus, wife of an American millionaire. She and her husband sat calmly side by side and waited for the ship to sink.

Of the 93 second-class women, 15 survived; out of 179 third-class, only 81 were saved. At one stage, the doors between the third-class quarters and the upper decks were locked to prevent people from surging on to the upper levels, but the passengers either knocked them down or pushed the seamen guards out of the way.

The men in first-class probably had little idea of the lack of assistance given to the 'lower order'. For the most part they observed 'women and children first' in strict honour. Benjamin Guggenheim and his valet disappeared to their cabins and returned in evening dress, once they saw the women off and knew there was no hope for themselves. They sat down in splendour to await their fate. Howard Case, a London oil executive, waved goodbye to his lady friends and was last seen leaning against the top deck sea rail, nonchalantly lighting a cigarette.

By the time most of the first-class women had got off the ship, the third-class passengers were still struggling to find their way up from the lower decks. Those aristocrats and magnates left contemplating their doom were astonished to see clusters of yet more women and children emerging from below. Some braver ones crawled up the escape ladders from the well deck aft; others found passageways through corridors rapidly filling with water and clambered over the side of the ship into the water.

While chaos reigned above, most of the crew below still had no thought of leaving the sinking ship. Between midnight and 2am, a desperate attempt was under way to pump boiler room 5 dry. Just when it looked as if the men would succeed, the entire bulkhead between rooms 5 and 6 gave way and the whole area was again flooded with icy water. One man managed to clamber up the escape ladder: another turned to help a mate with a broken leg and disappeared into the rising tide.

Radio man Phillips continued at his post frantically tapping out 'SOS' and details of the ship's position. Bride, the second in command, strapped on Phillips' life jacket without disturbing his work. Around 2.18 he had to fight off a desperate attacker who stole up behind the radio man, ready to rip the jacket off his back.

Finally the Captain gave the last order: 'Every man for himself', and the crew were freed from their responsibilities to the magnificent liner. The end was fast approaching. On the starboard deck one of the small collapsible lifeboats, 'C' was the last to be launched. Four crewmen and 45 passengers got in, including President Ismay. He was later criticized severely for saving himself when

he must have known that not all the passengers, not even all women and children, had got off.

1503 people were left to go down with the *Titanic*. Those lifeboats that got away safely could have picked up many of the wretched victims floundering all around in the cold ocean, but few stopped or turned back to pick up more people. Fifth Officer Lowe made the noblest effort. As his lifeboat approached four others, numbers 10, 12 and 4, and collapsible craft D, he gave orders to lash them together. He then circled around to pick up anyone he could find in the sea. He only saved four.

In Lifeboat Five, the women stoutly refused to accept an officer's suggestion that they row around searching, although they could not have been more than 300 yards from several swimmers whose cries could be heard across the waves. In Number Six, the situation was reversed: several first-class ladies implored their seaman to go back but he refused. In sorrow and silence they took turns rowing about four miles before they neared the rescue ships answering the SOS. It was a shameful episode. Of approximately 1500, only 13 people were pulled out of the water by 18 lightly loaded boats.

About 2.20am, the *Titanic* began her final dive into the Atlantic. At an almost perpendicular angle, she slid down into the waves. The ship's band, had stoically played a selection of ragtime tunes through the abandonment, but turned to an Episcopal hymn, *Autumn* (some say it was *Nearer My God to Thee*). As everything inside the vessel broke loose, there was an awe-inspiring roar, followed by silence. In the vortex created by the sinking *Titanic*, people in the sea were sucked under; others were flung off the decks and rails as

Above The iceberg carved a gash below the waterline in five of the ship's compartments.

Dramatic scenes from the last moments of the Titanic.
Big picture and right inset: *From one of the many films about the disaster "A Night to Remember".*
Left insert: *A drawing by Leo Jones Hyland, one of the ship's stewards, which he sketched quickly as he pulled away from the liner in one of the few lifeboats.*

she toppled over. That was the last of her. The boatloads of survivors turned their backs and pulled away into the night.

Aid was not long in arriving. Captain Rostron of the *Carpathia* had been so shocked by the SOS picked up from the *Titanic* that he radioed back to find out if it was 'absolutely certain' the liner was in distress. Once confirmed, the news was acted upon with all speed. The captain later confessed: 'When I saw the ice I had steamed through during the night, I shuddered and could only think that some other hand than mine was on the helm that night.'

One by one the lifeboats were sighted: between 4.45 and 8.30 they bobbed alongside the Cunard Liner, 705 survivors in all, including Ismay. He retired immediately to the ship's doctor's cabin and remained there until the ship docked in New York.

Meanwhile the *Californian* had seen the distress rockets sent up by the sinking ship, and her captain realized that those lights that had been spotted earlier were from the same vessel. At 5.40am, the wireless operator was summoned and

This page, above *The* Carpathia *braved the ice floes with a dramatic dash to reach survivors.*
Below *Survivors huddle on the deck of the rescue ship.*
Above right *The cause of the 'unsinkable' liner's destruction was a huge iceberg like this. Only about one ninth of its bulk is above water; the rest is hidden treacherously below the surface.*
Below right *There was no proper lifeboat drill on board the* Titanic, *unlike this scene where all the passengers escape a liner fire. Even if the ship had been better organized, many would still have died, for the* Titanic *carried only enough lifeboats for just over half the total number of passengers.*

ordered to open the radio channels and find out what had happened. Their horror can be imagined when it became clear that the greatest liner in the world had gone down less than 20 miles away, and they had known nothing about it.

In New York, news was received with equally stunned amazement. The White Star Line's offices were beseiged with anxious relatives, from the wealthiest to the poorest, wanting news. None came from the *Carpathia* until she docked four days later. 30,000 people waited on the waterfront.

Class distinction was maintained right through the aftermath of the disaster. The *New York American* newspaper devoted most of its coverage to millionaire John Jacob Astor, one of the first-class men who sat calmly waiting until he went down with the *Titanic*. The other 1800 lost were mentioned in a brief note at the foot of the front page.

At the Boards of Enquiry held in the USA and Britain, few witnesses from third-class were even called, let alone given fair attention, in spite of their accusations that they had been prevented from going up to the boat deck. Discrimination extended to 'foreigners': so many rude remarks were made by witnesses about the disorderly and cowardly behaviour of men passengers from below—'probably Italians, or some foreign nationality' as one put it, that the Italian Ambassador in New York demanded an official apology.

Although Bruce Ismay was severely chastized for saving himself by the American board, he was absolved by the British one, which concluded: 'Had he not jumped in he would merely have added one more life, namely his own, to the number of those lost.'

Blame was laid against the Captain and senior officers for failure to take notice of the four ice warnings that had been received. The Captain of the *Californian* was criticized for not going to the aid of the *Titanic*, though she was ice-bound and had her radio closed down for the night.

Worst of all was the lifeboat situation. Badly equipped, poorly positioned for launching and totally insufficient in number, they were the main reason for the loss of so many lives. The White Star Line was not legally to blame, but Bruce Ismay felt the moral burden, for he retired to Ireland soon after, living in virtual isolation until his death in 1937.

Could the *Titanic* disaster be repeated? It did bring about major reforms in passenger ship regulations. The required number of lifeboats was revised to cope with the maximum possible load. Boat drill became a rule. Perhaps more important, ship's radios must now remain open night and day to prevent a repeat of the *Californian*'s failure to respond. But there is no easy remedy for the most unforgivable aspect of the *Titanic* disaster: the disgraceful selfishness displayed by many of the survivors. Even in today's somewhat more egalitarian society, there might be some who would row away to safety, ignoring the cries of the helpless in an ice-bound sea.

May 22, 1922
Train crash at Quintinshill

Quintinshill Junction is unimportant as railway posts go, situated ten miles north of Carlisle, near Gretna Junction on the English–Scottish border. There were no peculiar weather conditions on the morning of May 22, 1915. It should have been a perfectly normal turn of duty for the two signalmen whose sole responsibility was manning the signal box there.

There are two main tracks at Quintinshill, one to the north, one to the south. In addition there are two 'loops': lay-by tracks on each side of the main line where trains can wait, parallel to the up and down lines.

In the early hours of that morning, two express trains had left Euston Station, London at 11.45

and midnight, and were both half an hour late by the time they neared Carlisle. As a result, another northbound train, a local from Carlisle, was sent to Quintinshill before the expresses, reversing its normal order. Because it provided a connection for Edinburgh and Glasgow at Beattock for passengers from Moffat, it had to keep to its schedule, and it was sent as far as Quintinshill so it would not lose too much time. There, it would wait in one of the loops until the expresses had gone through and could then proceed on its journey without much delay.

There was another unusual occurrence, unofficial and altogether secret. The night duty signalman, Meakin, was supposed to finish duty at

Below Burnt-out wreckage from the four trains involved in the Gretna Junction crash.

6am. But when he heard that the local from Carlisle was going to stop at Quintinshill, he stayed on the job, knowing that his relief, signalman Tinsley, would take advantage of an easy ride and come on the local from his home at Gretna Junction. Meakin covered up for his friend's late arrival by noting down all train movements and other messages received on a scrap of paper from 6 o'clock onwards. When Tinsley arrived, he would copy them into the official register, so that a different handwriting would appear at the right time. The system had worked without mishap several times before. After all, Quintinshill was not an important post.

The situation soon became more complicated. At 6.14am, Meakin saw the 4.50 goods train from Carlisle approaching. He arranged for this to wait in the down loop at the side of the main line. At 6.34 he signalled an empty coal train from the north into the lay-by on the up side. There were now only two lines of track free. With an alarming lack of foresight, Meakin instructed the local, just arrived, to switch to the up main line. It stood only 65 yards from his signal box, steaming merrily and awaiting further orders.

From the signal box at Gretna Junction, Meakin received word of the first approaching Scottish express, speeding on its way to make up for lost time. At this point, Tinsley appeared in the box to take over the daytime shift. As they exchanged a few words of greeting, another message flashed through, saying that a special troop train, carrying a regiment of the 7th Royal Scots to Liverpool, would soon be coming through Quintinshill. In other words, it was heading directly for the local, standing on the up main line. Neither Meakin nor Tinsley seemed perturbed by the quantity of early morning traffic coming their way. Meakin, in no hurry to rush off, settled down to read the morning newspaper supplied by Tinsley when he arrived. Two railwaymen from the goods trains parked in the loops appeared in the box to have a chat. Tinsley began writing up the entries he'd missed from 6 o'clock onwards in the big book, the Train Register.

Although the copying-up procedure was highly irregular, in this instance it meant that both Meakin and Tinsley were in a position to see their fatal mistake. Meakin should have realized that the local was blocking the line on which the troop train would be travelling. Even if he had a momentary lapse and overlooked it, Tinsley should have realized the error as he was copying up the entries.

In retrospect some spell seems to have been cast over these men to prevent commonsense from operating, for they were given yet another chance to remedy the confusion. 'Collars', supplied by the Railway Company, were to be dropped over the handles of the signal controls whenever a train blocked a main through-line to prevent a signalman from throwing the lever and giving an 'all-clear': no other train could pass on to that section of track while the collar was in place.

The fireman of the local came to check on the

position of his train, obediently following Rule 55 of railway regulations:

'If a train is held for more than three minutes, the fireman should visit the nearest box and confirm that the signalman is aware of the train's presence, and that proper precautions are taken'.

Fireman Hutchinson did not notice that the collar was not in place on the signal controls, nor did his arrival jog the memory of either Meakin or Tinsley about the position of the local and its now-impatient passengers.

At 6.38 Tinsley gave the signal for the approaching Scottish express from Euston. At 6.42 he gave the signal for the southbound troop train. Two minutes later the troop train, travelling very fast downhill on a gradient of 1-in-200, ploughed into the engine of the stationary local. The troop train was pulled by a four-coupled bogie express; the local by a No. 907, a heavy 4-6-0. The impact was tremendous. The coupling on the local broke, shooting the passenger carriages backwards for 136 yards. The engine ground back along the track for 40 yards and finally stopped half off the line, with its tender lying across the other main line. The troop train too turned sideways, blocking both tracks. The coaches of the troop train, packed with soldiers, were smashed to smithereens. Like many early 20th-century trains, the superstructures were made of wood. They splintered like matchsticks with the force of the impact. One carriage hurtled into the air, sailed over the engine and smashed to the ground in front of it. In one moment, a train 213 yards long was squashed,

Above Some of the 227 injured in the multi-collision received immediate aid in a field lying alongside the track.
Overleaf Only 52 men of the 7th Battalion of the Royal Scots were able to answer roll call the day after the crash. The other members of the unit, which had been 500-strong, were either dead or injured.

concertina-like, to a mere 67 yards long.

Injuries to the soldiers were appalling. Those who were stunned, dazed, but able, struggled to escape and help their comrades. As defenceless men began to think of rescue and safety, the Scottish express ploughed along the northbound line. Too late, Tinsley and Meakin realized what was going to happen. All the railwaymen who had been in the box ran hysterically along the track in a vain attempt to warn the express. One minute after the first collision, the express, weighing 600 tons, headed straight into the wreckage. The driver just had time to apply his brakes for a full emergency stop on the first of the express's two four-coupled bogies. But the sheer weight of the train bore it forward. It hit the troop train and drove its tender right through the wagons of the goods train standing on the down loop.

Survivors from the first collision had no chance. Within seconds the coal supply on the troop train ignited, probably due to the gaslight fixtures in the carriages, and flames lapped wildly over the mountain of iron and wood. Vain efforts were made to control the blaze with water pumped from a stream running through a nearby farm. Passengers who had escaped from the last carriages of the express train and the few soldiers left alive could do nothing to help those trapped

inside the carriages as the heat of the fire rapidly became intense and drove them back. Instead of supplying water to quench the blaze, the little farm became an improvized morgue for the bodies that could be extricated from the tangled mass of wreckage. Those who survived were laid in the flat field beside the train line to the east.

Most of the victims were Scottish soldiers on the way to the trenches in France. Because it was wartime, news coverage was limited and tried to hit a note of morale-boosting, even in the midst of unprecedented loss. The Quintinshill crash was the worst in British history, with 227 dead and 246 injured. But the newspapers concealed the horror under drum-beating: of the soldiers, it was reported, 'all had been in high spirits at the prospect of going to the front . . . They were men of magnificent physique, and they fought their road through the wreckage as though they had been called upon to storm a German trench.' But Private E Donald of the 2nd Life Guards who was travelling in the London express said soldiers 'who had been at the front said none of the scenes they had seen in the trenches were as bad'. Within days, the newspapers carried reports that a new regiment was to be raised immediately to replace the Quintinshill contingent at the front.

Hundreds of sightseers flocked to the site on

the Whitsun holiday that unfortunately came close after the disaster. There was plenty to see. The fire had blazed steadily all through the night after the crash. The Carlisle Fire Brigade had arrived at 10 that morning and struggled all day to control it, but by 9 o'clock the following day, 15 coaches of the troop train, four coaches of the express, five goods wagons and all the coal had gone up in flames. Even after breakdown gangs had been hard at work all day, a 100-yard stretch of track was still littered with débris—wheels retained their shape, strangely, but engine parts were distorted into unrecognizable lumps of gnarled metal.

Meakin and Tinsley were solely responsible for Quintinshill. Given safety precautions in existence at the time, they failed to do their duty. Both were sentenced to jail, the first for 18 months, the second for three years. But the memory of their failure was punishment enough. Both men had nervous breakdowns and were released after a year.

There were other precautions that could have been taken. Wooden superstructures are extremely unsafe especially for passenger transport. The troop train was made entirely of wood, even its under-frames. Gas lighting is extremely hazardous and probably made the fire catch more quickly and spread more energetically. There was also some doubt about the availability of crash equipment. The Scots soldiers had their own tools wagons coupled to their train; these were used to free survivors trapped in the wreckage. Without this chance event, many more lives would have been lost for lack of vital equipment.

Nowadays, important junctions are protected by being 'track circuited' at the joints. A section of track is insulated from adjoining sections. An electrically-operated switch is kept closed by a low-voltage current passing through the rails at all times. When a train runs over this part of the track, it 'short-circuits' the current, so that the switch opens. Even if the current fails by accident, the effect is the same. The movement of the switch is transmitted to the signal box: no other train can go on to that section of the line until it is cleared. A series of these circuits could effectively plot the progress of a train for its entire journey, although the system is too expensive to install everywhere.

That was the tragedy of Quintinshill. A small, unimportant junction would probably not have qualified for such sophisticated techniques. To work properly, the Quintinshill Junction depended on human skill, a quality all too absent on that May morning.

CANADA

NOVA SCOTIA

Halifax

ATLANTIC OCEAN

December 7, 1917
Explosion in Halifax harbour

Below Richmond, Nova Scotia, lay in ruins after the Mont Blanc *explosion.* **Inset** *The Belgian relief ship* Imo *collided with the ammunition ship.*

The French freighter *Mont Blanc* picked up a dangerous cargo in New York: 5000 tons of high explosives and combustible materials. The 3121-ton vessel was loaded with TNT, picric acid, gun cotton and barrels of benzene, ready for shipment to Europe. In December 1917 such supplies were vitally necessary for the war against the Germans—so necessary that the *Mont Blanc* was under orders to sail north to Halifax harbour, Nova Scotia, Canada, to meet up with the British cruiser, HMS *High Flyer*, which would lead the convoy safely across the Atlantic.

The *High Flyer* was already waiting in Halifax harbour when the *Mont Blanc* steamed in at about 9 o'clock on Thursday, December 6. Thin patchy fog made visibility a little difficult, but with a pilot on board, there was no cause for undue worry.

The harbour is six miles long with a breadth of about one mile, and affords secure deep-water anchorage at all times of the day, whatever the tide, for the largest ships afloat. But there is a point in the passage, called 'The Narrows', where the harbour slims down to a half-mile-wide channel. On the south shore lies the Richmond section of Halifax; on the north, the town of Dartmouth.

The pilot suddenly gave a mighty blast on his horn, for a ship was bearing down directly on the *Mont Blanc*—the outward-sailing Belgian relief ship, *Imo*. *Mont Blanc*'s captain gives an on-the-spot account of what happened next:

'The *Imo* signalled that she was coming to port which would bring her to the same side with us. We were keeping to starboard and could not understand what the *Imo* meant, but kept our course, hoping that she would come down as she should on the starboard side, which would keep her on the Halifax side of the harbour.

'. . . Then we put the rudder hard aport to try to pass the *Imo* before she should come on to us. At the same time the *Imo* reversed engines. As she was light, without cargo, the reverse brought her around slightly to port, her bow towards our starboard. As a collision was then inevitable, we held so that she would be struck forward of the hold where the picric acid substance, which would not explode, was stored, rather than have her strike where the TNT was stored'.

There was an almighty crash as the *Imo* sank deep into the *Mont Blanc*. Then, she reversed off desperately, while the sailors aboard the ammunition ship made a few frenzied efforts to scupper the *Mont Blanc* before the deadly cargo did any damage. But they soon realized that fire had already broken out where some of the benzene load had spilt on impact. A quick order came to abandon ship, and the crew obeyed, struggling to lower lifeboats and row as fast and as far away as they could.

On Pier 8, where the *Mont Blanc* should have docked, the fire alarm was raised. Halifax's one and only fire-fighting unit set out at full speed from the town, heading for the harbour. The Richmond telegraph operator Vincent Coleman also saw the fire and mistakenly telegraphed: 'A munition ship is on fire and is making for Pier 8. Good-bye.' He then hurried off to find his newly-wed wife.

The *Mont Blanc* crew got to shore and ran into the nearby woods. Suddenly it became clear that the ship was an enormous floating bomb, liable to explode at any second. People started to swarm out of dockside factories, offices and houses and scramble up the steep-sided cliff towards the historic Citadel building, Halifax's old fortress.

Another British ammunition ship, the *Pictou*, was already moored at Pier 8, and within seconds of the realization that the *Mont Blanc* would blow, she too was completely abandoned. Only the *High Flyer* took preventive action: the cruiser sent a boarding party in a launch with instructions to get to the *Mont Blanc* and sink her before anything terrible could happen.

But happen it did: about 15 minutes after the collision, the *Mont Blanc* drifting slowly towards the wharf, exploded in one enormous blast. An eye witness, William Barton, breakfasting at the Halifax Hotel, looked out at the scene in stunned realization:

'In ten seconds it was all over. A low rumbling, an earthquake shock, with everything vibrating, then an indescribable noise, followed by the fall of plaster, and the smashing of glass. A cry went up: "A German bomb".'

Through the smashed doors, survivors streamed out of the hotel and joined the panic-stricken multitude swarming up the harbour hillside to safety. The very geography of the place made the explosion all the more destructive, for the deep, high-sided channel contained the impact.

Damage to both life and property was immense. The blast was felt over 60 miles away. Half the city lay in ruins. The Intercolonial Railway Station, a brick and stone structure in downtown Halifax, was totally flattened, killing crowds of people waiting for trains on platforms or already seated in carriages. Schools too suffered great loss of life because at that hour—9.15am—everyone was assembled to begin lessons. Of 550 children in the Halifax area alone, only seven survived. The total number of people who died has never been established exactly, but conservative estimates put it at 1200, while others believe it may have been as great as 4000.

In the immediate harbour area, a large sugar-refining factory, the pier, the fire engine and its crew and almost all other buildings were completely destroyed. One hundred workers are known to have died in the refining plant.

The other area to suffer the greatest effect of the explosion was Richmond, across the harbour, because most of the houses were built of wood and clustered into narrow streets. The Richmond telegraph operator who ran for his wife was one

Right *Citizens of Halifax dig in the snow for bodies amidst the wreckage of the city. In the distance, the relief ship* Imo *flounders in the harbour.*

of those people who died. After the blast, the second great danger, fire, broke out here and in other parts of Halifax, and 25,000 people were made homeless.

Among the survivors, 5000 gathered in the open city common and were saved from further danger of explosion by the flooding of the naval ammunition depot near the Narrows, and by the courageous action of the Marine superintendent, J W Harrison, who got aboard the British ammunition ship *Pictou* and opened the sea valves. He set the vessel adrift, with water hoses playing over the decks, and within minutes the ship and all her cargo sank.

The Richmond telegraph operator's message was received in Moncton and St John. From the first a special train left at full speed, as early as 9.30, loaded with doctors, nurses, Red Cross helpers and all necessary medical supplies. Several more trains followed to take some of the homeless to shelter and to bring fire-fighting equipment.

The rescue effort was hampered by appalling weather conditions, for the morning fog worsened into driving snow and freezing temperatures. Wounded people lying amid the brick, rubble, shattered glass and charred wood had the added threat of exposure forced upon them. Electricity supplies were disrupted by the blast, so relief workers had to struggle in the increasing gloom, searching for the injured, who were rapidly becoming indistinguishable mounds in the snow among the dead.

On the outskirts of Halifax, people felt the tremor of the blast and saw the glass in their windows splinter and fly. The news came through to a girls' school, St Vincent's Academy, when a locomotive driven at full speed by one engineer arrived. He cried for help, bandages, clothes, anything, and the girls set about tearing up their uniforms to make dressings for the injured.

The snow had one beneficial effect: it suc-

ceeded in damping down the fires that had broken out. By afternoon, the danger had passed, but only wreck and ruin remained. A 2½-square mile area in the city centre was completely flattened.

Halifax city militia took command and declared martial law. More trains arrived with medical supplies and doctors and nurses from Boston and New York. All remaining public buildings, such as the Academy of Music, were opened to house the injured and the homeless. In the city common, the troops put up 500 tents for themselves and let women and children move into their barracks.

The explosion had the effect of bringing home to Canadians the full horrors of war. Previously the battles in Europe had been far away and only the movement of troops and war supplies reminded them of the dreadful struggle taking place in Europe. But *The Times* of London, ever mindful of the need to keep morale high at home took the opportunity to publicize the opinion of Lieutenant-Colonel Good of Fredericton, who said that he had never seen such a sight on the battlefields of France. 'All that could be seen for a great circumference were burning buildings, great mounds of iron and brick in the streets, and dead bodies'—anything that minimized the horror of the trenches was welcome to a British newspaper. But in Canada, unaccustomed to war on its doorstep, the disaster of Halifax harbour was doubly shocking: unexpected and unimagined. That was why the hotel guest thought the blast must have come from a German bomb. Nothing but a full-scale war offensive could explain the black pall of smoke that hung in the air—it must have been aerial attack. But, as the newspapers recorded, only 12 soldiers were killed at Halifax harbour. Thousands of civilians died; 8000 or more were injured and 3000 homes were destroyed. The true cause was not a planned act of aggression, but a momentary unthinking confusion over ships' signals.

JAPAN

Tokyo

PACIFIC
OCEAN

September 1, 1923
The Tokyo
Earthquake

Tokyo has often been afflicted by earthquakes, yet the superb location of the city on the mouth of the Sumida River, facing an enormous natural bay, has made it a centre of habitation for 4000 years. In the feudal era it was the beautiful imperial city of Edo, full of castles and moats; some of its old palaces and temples still stood at the beginning of the 20th century as reminders of the city's long cultural history and economic importance. But in 1923 Tokyo and the neighbouring port of Yokohama were devastated by Japan's worst earthquake, which almost wiped the ancient city and its people out of existence.

Because the warm mild climate and the Japanese style of living encourage houses built in flimsy structures out of simple wood panelling, the effect of the tremors were far worse than in San Francisco. The houses were simply flattened into firewood. The death toll was also infinitely greater. The earthquake happened in the middle of the day when the streets were full of workers going to lunch, and the coastal areas were

Below Yokohama, Japan's largest seaport, serving nearby Tokyo, immediately after the earthquake. Eighty percent of the buildings in the city were destroyed.

thronged with holiday-makers enjoying late summer sun and picnics in the parks.

At 11.58 on September 1, there was a violent tremor, followed by a second and a third. Seven prefectures of Tokyo were completely destroyed: Tokyo centre, Kanagawa, Shizuoka, Chiba, Saitama, Yamanashi and Ibaraki. Yokohama was also wiped out. The whole bay area was devastated.

In some areas, the land shifted up as much as eight or nine feet. The upheavals and depressions ran in a line from north to west and south to east between the Manazuru Peninsula and the Boso Peninsula, across Sagami Bay, in a direct path south of Tokyo itself. The most remarkable alteration in the landscape took place south of Yokohama, at the foot of the peninsula forming one of the arcs of Tokyo Bay. Just off Misaki, right at the tip, stands the island of Jogashima. The land there surged upwards with such force that the entire channel between the island and the mainland was laid bare, revealing hundreds of shell-covered rocks on what had been the ocean floor. During the first few days after the earthquake, land levels altered at the rate of two feet per day, until the final settlement stood five feet above the pre-quake height.

A second natural phenomenon caused instant heavy casualties: a *tsunami*, or tidal wave, lunged out of the sea at Atami on Sagami Bay, west of Yokohama, destroying 150 houses along the front and carrying off 60 people. The length of the giant tsunami from crest to crest may be more than 100 miles, and their height as little as two or three feet in open sea. They can pass through the ocean at speeds of up to 600 miles per hour. As they near the coast, they slow down, building up greater height, until they thunder on to the shore. So great is the force of a tsunami that, before it arrives, it causes the normal water line to recede dramatically or forces it forward to half again its usual height. Tsunamis are lethal; by the time an eye-witness has seen one build up on its run for the shore, it is too late for him to escape. The wave will overwhelm anyone and anything near enough to see it. The most common causes are vertical shifting in the sea bed, submarine avalanches or landslides on the ocean floor—or extended earthquake tremors. The first and third explanations might apply to the Sagami Bay disaster. At the time it was thought that the sea bed below the bay had sunk by as much as 40 fathoms, or 120 feet. Vertical displacement caused several waves along the coast, washing away many villages west of Tokyo and Yokohama.

The number of people who died in Tokyo as a direct result of the earthquake was comparatively few. Even so, the figures are high. A giant tower of the Asakusa temple crushed 700 people when it tumbled. Two great hotels in Yokohama, the Grand and the Oriental, collapsed almost instantly. In the rubble and the fire that followed 180 people, including 100 foreigners, died. Six hundred more were buried in a railway tunnel.

Below *Devastation in a Yokohama street.*

As in San Francisco, even greater calamity came with a monstrous conflagration that soon overwhelmed both Tokyo and Yokohama. All the water mains were dislocated and all electric cables snapped, so there was little hope of immediate aid when hundreds of small fires began to flare up within an instant of the third, and strongest, tremor. Most people had already lit their little charcoal and wood burners to make midday tea and rushed out of their houses in panic without thought of fire. The wind lifted, and as the heat of the fires increased, cyclones formed in the low-pressure atmosphere. Soon these swirling, circling mini-tornados swept across the city, spreading the fires uncontrollably.

By late afternoon an unusually strong cyclone built up in the northern part of the Sumida River and swept down its banks throwing small boats several feet in the air. It whirled over the burning school building at Kuramaye and sucked up a mass of flames, smoke and burning splinters. At Honjo, directly in its path, terrified refugees had gathered for safety, away from their shattered homes, in the grounds of a large clothing depot. The cyclone roared over the enclosure, setting it alight and suffocating everyone inside. All 40,000 perished in the blaze.

Downtown Tokyo presented a scene of devastation and confusion. Violent winds blew flames first this way, then that. There was no water to fight the fire. People ran screaming through the streets as quake-shaken buildings toppled about

them. Looting, arson, jail-breaks and other forms of civil disorder gripped the citizens in what the official report described as a 'reign of terror'. The police were completely unequal to the task of restoring calm. One strange aspect of reaction was that Korean residents in Tokyo (Japan had annexed their country in 1910) were somehow blamed for the violence and were so energetically persecuted that eventually special sanctuaries were set up for them at Narashino in Chiba Prefecture. More than 3000 Koreans fled for their lives.

The citizens of Tokyo gathered in the open spaces outside the Imperial Palace grounds and various other palaces and gardens throughout the day. Streets were jammed with anxious families pushing carts, carrying wicker baskets crammed with precious articles and clutching their children. Luckily as evening approached the air did not cool to a sharpness. They spent the night under the open sky without exposure. But food and water were severe problems. The army immediately donated a huge store of rice from a military provision depot at Etchujima, but before the city authorities could organize its collection, the building and its goods were destroyed by fire. Feverish activity began the same day on repairing broken water mains, and Tokyo was back on a limited supply by September 3, just two days later. Meanwhile, military vehicles and municipal water carts went round the refugee parks doling out small cupfuls to the thousands parched with thirst from

Below Many of Tokyo's ancient monuments were destroyed.
Overleaf Panic, looting and a total breakdown of law and order immobilized Tokyo in the aftermath of the 'quake.

the fire and smoke that surrounded them.

The panic grew so out of hand that martial law was officially declared on September 2. The Imperial Guard, the First Division of the Army and several infantry troops and engineer corps were sent to the area to help the police in organizing restoration of peace and order. The same day an emergency requisition ordinance went out and all supplies of food, fuel, medicines, vehicles and ships came under the control of a central Emergency Relief Bureau. The aim was to stop black-marketeering and share resources in the best possible manner.

In Tokyo, every major building was destroyed: 17 libraries, including that of the Imperial Palace, 151 Shinto shrines, 633 Buddhist temples and 202 Christian churches or missions were laid flat. Not one house escaped undamaged from the earthquake or the fire. In Tokyo Prefecture alone 59,000 people died, 10,900 were missing and 8700 were seriously injured.

Yokohama suffered equally severe devastation. It is situated in Kanagawa province, for which official records of the dead stood at 58,000, 21,000 of whom were in the port. Over 6000 people were injured and over 2000 lost. The total number of people killed or seriously injured in the whole region came to 156,693.

Yokohama had waked on September 1 to a rainy, gusty day, but by 10am the skies cleared and the crowds came out. Ten minutes before noon the earthquake hit. Mr Morioka, the Chief of Police, immediately set up headquarters in the central park and ordered out the fire brigades. He set out on a tour of inspection. The Customs House was ablaze, but nothing could be done as all available fire hydrants were broken. Large numbers of dead littered the streets. Survivors rushed towards the Park, but it had been turned into a quagmire by a burst water main and great rifts had appeared in the ground.

Along the river embankments and on city slopes, houses had slithered into the water. All roads were cracked and all bridges destroyed. By mid-afternoon Yokohama, like Tokyo, was in the grip of a conflagration made worse by high winds. At the docks, the warehouses at Nakamura, filled with explosives, roared and burst apart. People attempting to escape in tiny boats in the bay were soon caught as oil seeping over the water ignited.

When the police chief got back to Prefectural Building, which had survived the 'quake, he found it crammed with refugees but in imminent danger of catching fire from a blazing silk factory next door. He gathered up the people intending to head towards the Park, but now the streets were blocked with fire. The little crowd turned this way and that until it got to the quayside. In his own recollection, Mr Morioka described how the ground literally opened and shut in great cracks, so intense were the aftershocks that hit the region.

The crowd reached the quay, and the police chief had little alternative but to plunge into the oily water and swim to a nearby launch. He

ordered it to go to nearby ships, including the *Korea Maru,* and to pass the word to all bigger vessels to come alongside the quay and take off survivors. Thousands of people, backing on to the water's edge from the flaming city, were rescued by the combined efforts of the local ships. Morioka used the radio on the *Korea Maru* to send out one of the first messages about the earthquake to reach neighbouring areas:

'Today at noon a great earthquake occurred and was immediately followed by a conflagration which has changed the whole city into a sea of fire causing countless casualties. All facilities of traffic have been destroyed and communications cut off. We have neither water nor food. For God's sake, send relief at once.'

Without hesitation all cargo ships in the port of Yokohama offered their loads to help feed the starving survivors. When the news was received by the central government, two warships, *Yamashiro* and *Kasuga,* were dispatched to help.

Such was the confusion in the port, in particular on the old wharves leading into the main bay, that many ships were jammed into their moorings, and soon caught fire from sparks carried over from shoreline buildings. Many sailors jumped overboard in the burning sea or rushed on to the quayside where they soon lost their way in panic. By the end of the day the harbour master, who had been badly injured in the head, somehow

found his way to the port and got out to the *Korea Maru.* He soon set about reorganizing the berthing of the ships lying higgledy-piggledy all over the harbour.

Two great landmarks of Yokohama were destroyed by the disaster. The first was the long customs house pier that jutted far out into the harbour. This and the newly-built quayside provided deep mooring for liners coming to Japan from all corners of the world. Now the pier hung like a crumbling dead snake, pushed this way and that by the force of the 'quake.

The other monument was the Daijingu shrine, noted for its lovely groves of plum trees that blossom in February. Nothing remained but charred tree trunks and stone debris. The only reminder of former beauty was a small bronze statue of Li Kamon-no-Kami, a former minister-president who had done much to promote Yokohama as a prosperous centre of foreign commerce. The whole statue, pedestal and all, was completely turned round from north to east, as if moved by a giant hand.

Considering the total effect of devastation on Tokyo and Yokohama, it is a wonder that they ever recovered, but the energy that had turned the area into one of the world's greatest ports and commercial centres soon reasserted itself. The first news of the disaster reached Osaka on the evening of the first day and through the night the Army Aviation Headquarters sent planes to reconnoitre the area and report exactly what was happening and what relief was immediately needed.

Within the next few days a novel method of communication helped Tokyo to get the outside equipment and services so desperately needed. A special carrier pigeon corps was organized by the army and formed a dispatch service between Nikko (where the Imperial villa was situated), Chiba, Osaka, Odawara and other towns nearby.

The worst problem was housing and shelter. After a week, there were still 13,000 people in the Imperial Palace grounds, 5200 near Tokyo Station, 5600 in Hibiya Park, and 2000 near Municipal headquarters. The army lent tents and put up barracks to provide temporary accommodation, but the government report on the earthquake noted that every effort was being made to get rid of them as soon as possible. Within weeks, because they were hurriedly built and took in refugees irrespective of their means and occupations, there were wide differences in the condition of occupants, leaving much to be desired from both morale and sanitary points of view.

Disease was a further hazard after the earthquake, with epidemics of dysentery, typhoid and other illnesses causing the death of another 3705 people.

But the Japanese spirit began to pull the citizens of Tokyo through. First, railway and steamship companies volunteered transport to take away refugees. Two million left by September 16, easing the burden on the emergency network. From September 6 large supplies of food began to arrive in the city from the surrounding country-side, helping to restore the normal routine of family life. Street markets re-opened and mothers could go shopping. For two weeks after the earthquake, what little public transport could operate was run free for all citizens, but the administrators did not allow easy charity to continue for long. After the 16th, passengers had to produce a special certificate to prove they were 'earthquake sufferers' to get the concession.

These moves helped the citizens to regain their sense of place and independence. Their worst problem was insurance, because nearly all shopkeepers, house owners and business owners had overlooked a standard clause in most local insurance schemes, exempting the protected party in case of earthquake. The government finally stepped in and set up aid schemes so most people could claim at least enough to make a fresh start. In the USA, President Coolidge and the Red Cross began a fund with a $5,000,000 target figure; within a few days twice that amount was received and donated. Other nations sent money, ships, supplies and medical teams in the months that followed.

Tokyo's recovery was impressive. It faced fresh calamity in the heavy air-raids made by American bombers in World War II, but by 1970, its population had increased to 22,000,000 in the urban area, and it has become the centre of Japan's financial and industrial life, overtaking Osaka. But the threat of devastation by earthquake is ever-present and seemingly without any hope of a cure.

Above *A tidal wave or 'tsunami' swept into Sagami Bay, west of Yokohama, destroying 150 homes and killing 60 people. Tsunami are not caused by the moon's course but by earthquake tremors or shifts in the sea bed many miles offshore. They reach a maximum speed of 600 miles per hour. Today, advance warning systems give people time to reach higher ground.*

FRANCE
Beauvais
Paris

October 5, 1930
The crash of
the R101

First officer of R101, Lieutenant Commander Atherstone, made an entry in his diary, the day before the R101 crash:

'Everybody is rather keyed up now, as we all feel that the future of airships very largely depends on what sort of show we put up. There are very many unknown factors and I feel that that thing called "Luck" will figure rather conspicuously in our flight. Let's hope for good luck and do our best . . .'

Amid cheers from a large crowd gathered in the fields below at 6.36 on October 4, 1930, the R101 left her mooring tower at Cardington, north of London, and set out on her maiden voyage for India. Aboard were the cream of aviation development engineering—men like Atherstone, Major G H Scott, Colonel Richmond, Wing Commander Colmore, and the Captain, Flight Lieutenant Irwin, one of the most senior and experienced airship flyers in the country. Some prominent civil service officials were also present, pleased at last to take part in this historic journey—Sir Sefton Brancker, Director of Civil Aviation at the Ministry, and Lord Thomson, Secretary of State for Air. Six officials from the Royal Airship Works and Lord Thomson's valet brought the total to 54 people. First stop was to be Ismailia,

The R101 rests at her mooring at Cardington, ready for her maiden voyage to India. With this flight the Air Ministry hoped to inaugurate a new Commonwealth transport service.

Suez Canal.

As the R101 moved steadily south, she sent out regular radio messages so that her course could be followed. She circled over Bedford, then rose to 1000 feet, then to 1500 feet as she moved towards London. As the airship left her mooring, she gave a slight lurch, so Irwin ordered water ballast to be dropped at once. A warning from the meteorological office had told him to expect winds of up to 40 to 50mph, worse than any conditions a British airship had experienced over land in the past.

As the ship passed over Hitchin, Hertfordshire, a housewife was horrified to see it so low in the air; it barely cleared the trees around her home. She could see into the airship quite clearly. There the distinguished passengers were enjoying a celebratory dinner, and the candelabra were gleaming on snow-white tablecloths.

At 8.21pm the airship reported, 'Over London. All well. Moderate rain . . . course now set for Paris.' The message also gave the wind speed as 25 miles an hour—less than anticipated. As the ship passed over the Channel, a moderately serious engine problem occurred, but by the time R101 reached the French Coast the engineers had corrected it. The winds picked up over the sea, and the airship slowly lost height, until it reached the alarmingly low level of about 750 feet. At 10pm, the height coxswain (whose sole responsibility was maintaining correct altitude) received a visit from Lt Commander Atherstone, who took over the wheel himself for a while until considerable increase in height had been achieved. Then he handed back the controls to the coxswain, warning him not to let the R101 go below 1000 feet again.

At 11pm the watch was changed, and the night crew came on duty. At midnight, the airship sent out a further message. In spite of the rough weather conditions and serious trouble in maintaining height, its words betrayed no real fears on the part of the airship's guests and crew:

'After an excellent supper our distinguished passengers smoked a final cigar and having sighted the French coast have now gone to bed to rest after the excitement of their leave-taking. All essential services are functioning satisfactorily. The crew have settled down to watch-keeping routine.'

R101 sent out regular position reports at 1.28 and at 1.51, by which time she was approaching Beauvais, north of Paris. As she passed slightly to east of the town, many people heard the drone of her engines, and those who had been awaiting the sound rushed to the windows to catch a glimpse of this historic sight: the vast silver-white cigar-shaped dirigible floating over their heads with its warning lights twinkling, buffeted by rain and storm clouds.

Just outside Beauvais, with no warning at all, the R101 went into a steep dive. It tilted so sharply that the engineers manning the ship were thrown off-balance, and furniture shot forward

across the decks. The height coxswain pulled hard on his wheel in an effort to right the ship and got the airship once more to its proper height. But within seconds the ship lunged downwards again and this time the cox could do nothing to pull her out of the dive.

The officers in command could see what was coming. They ordered all engines to be cut dead, although only one was stopped, and warning bells were rung. It is difficult to imagine, but there was no panic. Airship flight is normally so smooth and buoyant and altitude changes so much a part of the pattern, that few people would leap to the idea of 'crashing' in the way that modern aircraft might. The chief coxswain had time to go aft, where the crew were sleeping, to announce quite matter-of-factly, 'We're down, lads.'

With a great grinding noise of engines ceasing and metal grating on metal, the airship lumbered to the earth and slid several yards along the ground. Then it burst into flames: the bags of hydrogen, the gas that kept it afloat, roared up instantaneously on ignition. Only one man actually saw the R101 catch fire—Eugene Rabouille, a local factory worker out hunting rabbits, described the last moments of this great enterprise:

'I clearly saw the passengers' quarters, well-lit, and the green and red lights on the right and left of the airship. Suddenly there was a violent squall. The airship dipped by the nose several times, and its forepart crashed into the northwest edge of the Bois des Coutumes. There was at once a tremendous explosion, which knocked me down.

'Soon flames rose into the sky to a great height—perhaps 300 feet. Everything was enveloped by them. I saw human figures running about like madmen in the wreck. Then I lost my head and ran away into the woods.'

The sight of the helpless dying is not one to attract a man caught by surprise: of the 54 people on board, seven escaped. They were extremely lucky. Most of the survivors were in the engine car, where one of the water ballast tanks burst, inundating it. This protected the six men there from the intense heat of the surrounding fire and

Left The interior structure of the R101, showing the massive steel frame required to support the 17 gasbags that gave the airship its lift. *Above* A sample of the elegant fittings inside the R101. On her maiden voyage the airship was carrying the top men of British aviation.

gave them a few seconds' grace. They jumped through a small opening, the port quarter on the lefthand side of the stern. Harry Leech, the only official from the Royal Airship Works who survived, got away by hacking a hole in the passengers' 'smoking room' and literally jumping through the burning body of the ship. He landed in the branches of a tree, and as it was raining, the leaves showered water all over him. In his own laconic words, this 'cooled me off'.

Next day, nothing remained of the glorious R101 but a massive tangle of scorched metal. What bodies could be found were brought back to London for a memorial service at St Paul's Cathedral and a requiem mass at Westminster Cathedral before removal to their final resting place, a communal grave at Cardington. Later, a memorial was built at the site of the crash at Beauvais.

What caused the destruction of the R101, and the appalling loss of so many adventurous and talented men? The R101 was built of dreams, and with its end, British airship hopes vanished.

Airships had been pioneered by the German inventor Count Von Zeppelin. Together with Dr Hugo Eckener, he set up the Zeppelin Company, which between 1910–14 made more than 2000 flights carrying 10,000 or more passengers in their first four ships, the *Schwaben, Viktoria Luise, Hansa* and *Sachsen*. Most of these flights were local, not more than about two hours long.

The basis of airship construction is simple. Large balloons containing lighter-than-air gas, either hydrogen or helium, were strapped around a metal inner structure where the cabins, decks and engine rooms were housed. Around the whole, a large cigar-shaped outer skin was pulled tightly into place. The gasbags provided the lift; engines provided the forward motion. Large bags of water ballast were added so height could be regulated by dropping weight as the ship rose. As it climbed higher scoops on the outside envelope collected rainwater or condensation from wet clouds, so that water-weight could be renewed during the flight. The emergency ballast bags were shaped like trousers, called 'lederhosen' by the Zeppelin crews. If the ship came down too low during a flight, the height coxswain pulled a lever on his control panel. The water bags could be emptied in a matter of seconds, as the R101 had done almost immediately after take-off.

The first British models were close copies of the Zeppelins. A German airship, the L33, was captured in 1916 when it made a forced landing in Essex. From it, the British evolved the R33, R34 and R38. In 1919 the R34 made a successful return journey across the Atlantic, and the R33 completed a total of 800 hours' flying without mishap. The R38 was less fortunate. On August 24, 1921, it broke in two while maneuvring in mid-air, travelling at its maximum speed of 60 miles an hour, and plummeted into the Humber River. Forty-four lives were lost. The fault appeared to lie in R38's construction. No allowances had been made for the stresses and strains

set up by steering the airship at high speeds. A great deal still had to be learned about airship design and constuction.

It seems strange today that 60mph should be considered fast, but the outstanding feature of airships was their speed related to their enormous size. While small two-seater aircraft could zip along at several hundred miles an hour in the 'twenties, no one could conceive of jumbo jets. Heavier-than-air planes were seen as limited passenger carriers, whereas the great airships could accommodate 20 to 50 people at a time. Aeroplanes generally made short hops and did not do much night-flying. The airships could maintain a steady 60mph night and day and did not need to land often for refuelling. So even the R38 disaster did not stop imaginative minds from contemplating a great airship future.

The ultimate scheme came from Sir Samuel Hoare when he was Secretary of State for Air. He planned a transcontinental fleet of airships to link all the countries of the Commonwealth, to bind them together in a closer political and social union than had ever been contemplated. Airships would allow freer travel; news and ideas would spread swiftly, and trade would improve immeasurably, as airships had great potential as cargo carriers as well.

With this in mind, two airships were ordered in 1928: the R100 and the R101. The R100 was built as a private enterprise, inspired by the leading British supporter of lighter-than-air vehicles, Sir Dennistoun Burney. Its manufacture was in the hands of the Airship Guarantee Company, a subsidiary of Vickers. Reputedly to prevent this firm's getting a monopoly in the air as it had with submarine development, the Government decided to build the other ship, the R101, under its own authority and set up a 'rival' concern at Cardington—the Royal Airship Works.

Almost at once, disparities appeared between the two organizations. R100 had the best designer in the country, B N Wallis, who was later responsible for the Wellington bomber and the dambuster bomb. The government project at Cardington had at its head Lt-Colonel Vincent Richmond. He had considerable experience with balloons and with German airship technique, but less practical knowledge than Wallis. At a personal level, however, the two teams had close, if competitive, relationships.

Sir Samuel Hoare organized the building of various mooring towers to link up his projected Commonwealth service. The earliest were erected at Ismailia in Egypt, Karachi, India and Montreal, Canada. Each mast was a major task, higher than Nelson's column and fitted with a lift, searchlights, spiral staircase and winches to pull the ships into position. There were underground fuel tanks holding 10,000 gallons of diesel oil, with a pump capable of raising the fuel to a height of 400 feet. Other pumps were installed to supply 5000 gallons of water an hour. Each tower, 200 feet high and 70 feet across at the base, could withstand a pull of 30 tons in any direction at the

top and cost £50,000 to build.

However, the government project at Cardington, paid for by public money, always had to cut corners. Although steel was used for the frame instead of duralumin, which had been used in the R38, the same problematic fabric was used for the gasbags. In these days of synthetic materials in seemingly endless varieties, it is difficult to imagine the difficulties and limitations faced by the R101 team. For their gasbags they used 'goldbeaters' skin', made from the membrane of bullock's intestines laboriously stitched together. The skins were imported from the Chicago cattle market, and it is estimated that more than a million animals supplied the fabric for the R101 bags.

Hundreds of wires held the 17 gasbags in position around the frame. During test runs, the bags seemed to chafe against the metal structure, so 4000 special cushions were added to prevent any further damage to them. New valves were especially designed so the amount of gas in the bags could be carefully controlled. Unfortunately, they

were so sensitive that an unexpected roll or lurch in the airship would make them release gas. The ship could easily lose height at a time when it did not intend to.

All these relatively minor problems were the kind of design-and-development headache that might be anticipated with any ambitious project. Given time, most of them would be corrected.

But the R101 had no time. In 1929 when the Government changed, Lord Thomson became Secretary of State for Air. He too was an airship enthusiast, and he decided on a magnificent launching trip for the government's project at Cardington. He would fly in the R101 to India himself in the autumn of 1930.

Thomson has been subsequently blamed by many experts for putting pressure on the R101 team. He felt that in a public venture, there should be some demonstration of confidence and success before too much money and time had been spent. He maintained before the flight that he deferred to the experts' opinion on progress and would never countermand their wishes nor

Above left *The R101 in action. The airship threw out water ballast as she rose from the mooring tower.*
Below left *French officials examine the twisted metal wreckage of the airship where she crashed, just north of Paris at Beauvais. There were only seven survivors out of the 54 men on board.*

53

put public relations before individual safety.

On the other hand, the R101 team came under a great deal of pressure from the success of their rivals, the R100 team. That ship had been launched in December 1929. Although she proved heavy (about seven tons over), she was very manouverable and a fast flyer, reaching 80mph top speed. On July 29 the following year, the R100 left on a round trip to Canada and back. Though the outer covering fabric was ripped twice during storms, the ship's general performance was admirable. The R100 tried diesel engines, like the R101, in the early stages, but gave them up and went back to Rolls Royce Condor aero-engines. These weighed nine tons in comparison with the R101's seventeen, although the R100 had to carry correspondingly more fuel to cover the same distance.

There is no doubt that the success of the R100 added steam to the R101 efforts at Cardington, where the whole team was anxious to prove that their airship was as good, if not better. Her first flight had been made in October 1929, but her major public showing took place during the Royal Air Force Display at Hendon on June 28, 1930. The great airship flew low over the heads of the crowd at about 500 feet. Little did the excited airship enthusiasts watching realize that the R101 had in fact gone into a steep dive, only pulled out by swift, skilful handling by the coxswain.

The ship was flying 'heavy': something had to be done before the well-publicized trip to India could take place on schedule three months later. It was decided to split the ship in two and add an extra bay, to give greater volume. The ship's diameter at its maximum was 132 feet; its capacity 5,508,800 cubic feet; its gross lift 167·2 tons. R100 kept to its original size, 144,400 cubic metres. After the disaster, this difference led to heated argument over the wisdom of increasing R101's length.

In those final hectic months, the ship was not only stretched but a whole new outer skin was sewn in place. The airship was ready on September 25. Foul weather looked as if it would postpone the final test flights until October, but the skies cleared enough on September 30 for a last-minute trial run.

Immense debate has centred on the thoroughness of the final tests. It is held by some experts that vital reports on the R101's airworthiness were not complete when the Air Ministry issued the appropriate Certificate on October 2, without which the flight to India could not take place. The verdict of the Court of Inquiry on this point was: 'The R101 started for India before she could be regarded as having emerged successfully from all the exhaustive steps proper to the experimental stage.'

It is extraordinary that after all the efforts to lighten the ship by lengthening it and jettisoning some non-vital mechanical devices, the R101 set off on her first official voyage bulging with bric-a-brac. Pale blue Axminster carpeting was laid in the passengers' quarters; silver dining sets and cutlery were put aboard. Elegant potted palms dotted the bamboo-furnished lounge and smoking room. The luxury of the fitments can hardly be imagined in the modern age of streamlined plastic jet-travel. To compensate for additional weight, the crew had left their parachutes behind. How could wool carpeting remain?

Publicity was partly to blame, for at the Imperial conference in London in November 1929, when the airship service had been announced, one reporter proudly claimed: 'The R101 will provide luxuries undreamed of by Jules Verne and H G Wells. It will positively be an aerial hotel.'

General conclusions on the cause of the R101 disaster centre around its weight, although the exact finding of the Court of Enquiry, published on April 1, 1931, was that the airship came down with a sudden loss of gas in a forward gasbag at a time when the nose of the craft was being depressed by a downward current of air.

> 'In the construction of the R101 the designers broke away almost completely from conventional methods . . . originality and courage in design are not to be deprecated, but there is an obvious danger in giving too many separate hostages to fortune at one time.'

So much faith and confidence had been placed in the R100 and R101 that at first newsmen on night duty refused to believe the reports of the Beauvais crash. Only the *Express* ran the story in their Sunday edition. The shock of the disaster was so great that it put a stop to further airship development in the UK. The R100 (ironically the more successful in design and performance) was kept on the ground for a year, finally broken up and sold for scrap at £400. Worse still, so many talented men died in R101 that the development of civil aviation in Great Britain was set back years. No comparable disaster has hit any industry in quite the same way, before or after R101.

There can be no doubt that political necessities behind the R101 affected its development. Harry Leech, the survivor who landed in a tree, went to work for Sir Malcolm and Donald Campbell later in their efforts to break water and land speed records. He commented, 'One thing R101 proved is that politics and experimental work don't mix.' Another conclusion is that the R101 project was too fraught, too ambitious. Dr Hugo Eckener, the great Zeppelin expert, was once shown the plans for the R101. 'Very nice', he said, 'but isn't it a little big?' The final word of judgement came from the Court of Enquiry:

> 'It is impossible to avoid the conclusion that the R101 would not have started for India on the evening of the 4th October if it had not been that reasons of public policy were considered as making it highly desirable for her to do so if she could.'

In spite of Lord Thomson's protests, political expediency was to blame.

Right The smoking stern of the Morro Castle lies beached at Asbury Park, New Jersey. On the quayside stands a fascinated crowd of local residents.

September 8, 1934
Fire on the
Morro Castle

There are few stories of sea disasters that can
match that of the *Morro Castle* for mystery and
sheer human stupidity. Error upon error resulted
in the total destruction of the 11,520-ton vessel
and the loss of 134 lives.

September 7, 1934: the Ward Line cruiser
Morro Castle was speeding along the east coast of
the USA, bound for New York. It was near the
end of a successful trip to Havana, and passengers
were busily exchanging addresses and packing
their souvenirs.

Last-night celebrations were marred by the
sudden illness of the Captain. Late in the evening
he had complained of stomach pains and within
an hour was found dead in his cabin. Captain
Robert Willmott was only 55. The senior ship's
surgeon, Dr De Witt Van Zile, could only find
'acute indigestion' as the cause of death.

Willmott's close friend and chief officer,
William Warms, assumed command of the ship.
His first duty was to send a message to the Ward
Line offices, informing his employers of the
Captain's death. Then he checked the ship's
course. The *Morro Castle* was approaching New
Jersey, her powerful turbo-electric engines
pounding through stormy seas. The *Scotland
Lightship* and the New York channel lay ahead.
The liner was keeping to her time schedule and
proceeding normally.

Below, however, things were far from calm. A
small fire had broken out in the passengers'
library and writing room. At first three sailors
tried to cope with the blaze themselves. (Almost
exactly 30 years later a similar fire broke out on
the *Lakonia*, and the same stupid mistake was
made—crew tried to put out the blaze by themselves before warning the captain officially. In
both cases, precious fire-fighting time was lost.)
In the case of the *Morro Castle*, the incident was
not an isolated one. A fire in her hold on a previous trip had been blamed on Cuban communist
agitators or some criminal element of New York's
rough waterfront population.

The sailors found they could not control the
fire. Before long, curls of smoke were creeping
silently along the deck corridors. The ship's
owners had made great publicity of the *Morro
Castle*'s modern fire-proofing systems, yet no
general alarm sounded, and the crew were totally
unable to check the fire's spread.

The chief radio operator George Rogers was
summoned from his bunk by his assistant George
Alagna. Realizing the fire was spreading, Rogers
went to his post at the radio and sent Alagna to the
bridge to see what instructions he could get from
the acting captain, Warms. Minutes ticked by and
no news came back. Rogers dispatched his second
assistant Maki with the same message: 'Find out
what signals they want me to send'.

By now, smoke was billowing along all the corridors, yet no word came from the bridge. Warms
must have assumed that his crew would even-

tually gain control of the fire. Perhaps his thoughts were wandering with the Captain's death weighing on his mind. Whatever led to his lack of decision, the *Morro Castle* continued on her course at full speed, 21 knots, with the disastrous effect of fanning the fire like a huge natural bellows. Soon all the deck structures were lapped with tongues of flame.

The time was now about 3am. Awakened by the smell of burning, passengers began to mill about the decks and corridors. There was no official announcement, and no message was sent out via the crew to get the passengers into the lifeboats.

At 3.13 Rogers heard a message on his radio. A nearby ship, the *Andrea Luckenbach*, was calling the shore station and asking if there was news of a ship on fire nearby—they could see smoke rising above the waves. Rogers, having no instructions about sending any definite message, could only tap out a 'stand by' signal, 'CQ' which he repeated three times. Once again he sent Alagna, his assistant, for orders from the bridge. Alagna was impatient with running about and was getting desperate. He did not think anyone on the bridge could give a satisfactory answer, and by now most crew and passengers were concerned only with escape.

The *Andrea Luckenbach*, the *Monarch of Bermuda*, the *President Cleveland*, the *City of Savannah*, the coastguard cutter *Tampa* and a

navy destroyer, USS *Chester*, converged on the *Morro Castle* in answer to Roger's messages. Now passengers began to jump overboard to save themselves from the blaze. Launching the lifeboats was chaotic and slow. People got so desperate that they preferred to trust themselves to the mercy of the waves than stand about choking in the smoke and heat of the rapidly burning decks. One crewman from New York, Leroy C Kelsey, described the scene:

'Black smoke poured down stairways and there was a rush of running feet. Flames cracked and roared and the black windows were shot with red and yellow gleams—were there people in there? We were trapped on the port side of the dying ship; three girls, too young to die, myself and several men in the uniform of the steward's department.'

Whole families went overboard together, like the Phelps—a New York doctor, his wife and 25-year-old son. Two sisters, Gladys and Ethel Knight, went over the side, Ethel clutching a small 7-year-old boy, Benito Rueda of Brooklyn. Luckily the water was warm, and the waves helped to push people in towards the New Jersey shore.

At last, at 3.20, Warms gave the signal for Rogers to send the SOS message, now hopelessly overdue. A few lifeboats were lowered on the starboard side. On the port side, flames were too

Above The ocean liner remained stranded at Asbury Park for several months. Eager tourists paid for admission tickets to get a close look at what was left of '*The pride of the Havana run*'.

Overleaf The cause of the Morro Castle *blaze remains a mystery. The official enquiry could only state it as* '*spontaneous combustion*'.

intense for anyone to get near. Rogers continued at his post, sending out details of position, '20 miles south of Scotland Light'. His last message: 'Hurry, can't hold out much longer', came just before the generator exploded in the heat.

Alagna got hold of Rogers, by now in a semi-collapsed state, and together they stumbled along the decks and corridors to the bridge. Eight lifeboats got away; only 15 people including Warms and Rogers remained on board the blazing liner. About 4am, the *Andrea Luckenbach* neared the scene of the disaster and picked up 11 persons flailing about in the open sea. Then the *President Cleveland* arrived. It launched two lifeboats and searched for one and a half hours but found no survivors. The *City of Savannah* picked up one, Margaret Cotter of Springfield, Massachusetts, who had kept afloat for five hours. A coastguard boat from New Jersey gathered 70 souls and ferried between the ocean and the *Luckenbach* with its load, searching again and again for more.

Some people actually managed to reach the shore unaided, crawling exhausted on to the beach at Sea Girt. Local residents, watching the smoke billows of the flaming *Morro Castle*, ran forward to help them. The two sisters, Gladys and Ethel Knight (still clutching Benito) were nearly ashore when they were rescued by small boats.

As usually happens after a disaster, crowds flocked to the scene to watch the end of the *Morro Castle*. This was one of the first tragedies to involve extensive 'action' news coverage. Scores of light planes hovered over the burning wreck transmitting live reports for radio and newspapers, helping to swell the crowd at Asbury Park, the New Jersey town near where the *Morro Castle* lay floundering in the rough ocean.

Of the 318 passengers, 90 died; of the 231 crew, 44. Some reports claimed that the crew behaved badly, saving their own skins and neglecting their duty to assist the rest. But the main blame must lie with the officers who apparently did nothing to command obedience or create disciplined escape procedures and quell panic. The evidence of the lifeboats is damning. One was lowered with 13 aboard, another with three. The capacity of each was 70. Only eight lifeboats with 85 persons in them were pulled ashore.

The coastguard cutter *Tampa* attempted a salvage operation of the *Morro Castle*. All day Saturday, September 8, crowds watched in fascination as the cutter laboured to tow the hulk past Sea Girt and up to New York harbour. As senior coastguard officer, Captain Earl Rose had power to order Warms, the acting captain, and the few remaining crew, including radio man Rogers, to leave the ship. There was not much left of the *Morro Castle*. A reporter from the London *Daily Express* filed this graphic description viewed from an aeroplane circling above the wreck:

'. . . Flaming patches of oil floated on the surface of the sea. Great clouds of steam went up

from the water's edge . . . All the superstructure was burnt. The funnels just melted away in the intense heat.'

The *Tampa* had to give up the struggle to tow the *Morro Castle* to a safe mooring: the sea had roughened again and the weight of the liner was slowly pulling the cutter towards the beach. The towline finally broke and (to the delight of the sightseers) the *Morro Castle* fell away into the surging waves and came to rest on the shore at Asbury Park. It remained a tourist attraction for months, with visitors buying tickets to come and stare at what had once been 'The pride of the Havana run'. It was finally towed to Baltimore for scrap in March 1935.

The enquiry put the cause as 'spontaneous combustion'. No one established how the fire started, although it may have been caused by the ship's funnel which passed very close behind the library wall near the start of the fire, overheating the wood panelling of the room. A federal court found Chief Officer Warms and Chief Engineer Abbot guilty of misconduct, negligence and failure to their duty, but they were spared prison sentences on appeal.

A bizarre story surrounds the radio officer George Rogers. He was considered a hero for sticking to his post and contacting other vessels in spite of a lack of clear orders from the bridge. He joined a New Jersey police force, but was later convicted of planting a bomb with intent to injure his superior officer. After 11 years, he was back in prison, this time on a charge of murder, for which he received a life sentence. He had a criminal record dating back to the age of 12.

An American author, Thomas Gallagher, wrote a dramatic reconstruction of the *Morro Castle* disaster, published shortly after Rogers died in 1958. Gallagher tried to show that Rogers murdered the Captain and set fire to the ship deliberately. There is little beyond flimsy circumstantial evidence and Rogers' criminal background to support the theory. The ship's doctor, who died in the flames, could not even be questioned on the exact cause of the Captain's death.

The enquiry found two clear explanations for the rapid spread of the fire. First, the ship, designed as it was for cruises in warm tropical seas, had an open-deck construction that allowed the flames to spread easily from deck to deck. Also, Warms had allowed the liner to continue her course at between 18 and 20 knots in a high wind, with the obvious effect of whipping up the flames even more.

The *Morro Castle* disaster continued to affect people's lives long after the event. Chief Officer Warms went back to sea as second officer on another ship, the *Cauto*, which foundered in the Gulf of Mexico. He never eluded the taint of catastrophe that seemed to haunt him. Ethel Knight, who had saved 7-year-old Benito Rueda, married soon after, but died of a heart attack four weeks later. The Massachusetts Humane Society awarded her a silver medal, posthumously.

Right A coastguard acting commander returns to shore with another victim of the fire. Of 318 passengers, 90 died; of 231 crew, 44 were lost.

60

USA

New York

ATLANTIC OCEAN

May 6, 1937
The burning of the Hindenburg

The Hindenburg was a landmark in passenger transport; the culmination of a lifetime's work for two airship experts of world renown, Dr Hugo Eckener and Count von Zeppelin. She was the largest and most elegant lighter-than-air craft ever designed. 814 feet long with a maximum diameter of 135 feet, she cruised at a steady 80 knots, driven by four 100-horsepower Daimler diesel engines. Inside her frame a total of 14 miles of metal bracing supported her, with buoyancy supplied from 16 gasbags filled with hydrogen.

On her lower deck, the crew accommodation, the kitchens, the officers' dining-room, bars, showers and a ballroom were built along the centre spine of the ship. Above, on the 'A' deck were 25 splendid state-rooms, fitted with luxurious carpeting, drapes and bed covers, with wash-basins, wardrobes and mirrors. On the port side of the top deck was the passengers' dining-room and promenade; on the starboard side a lounge with a grand piano. A reading and writing room and another promenade completed the interior.

Launched on March 4, 1936, the Hindenburg soon passed all her test runs and successfully completed her maiden voyage to South America. In that year she made seven voyages to Brazil and ten to the USA, mooring at Lakehurst, New Jersey, south of New York. To travel her was the height of style, and the transatlantic fare was so enormous that only high society and the world's self-made men could even contemplate the trip. Even so, there was a long waiting list of would-be passengers. So great was the German Zeppelin Company's confidence in the Hindenburg that in the winter of 1936, the airship was temporarily removed from service to be refitted to take even more passengers. Eleven extra cabins were added, bringing the maximum passenger capacity to 72.

Dr Hugo Eckener, the ship's designer, was unhappy about one of the Hindenburg's first duties after the alterations were completed. Goebbels, the Nazi propaganda chief, had insisted that the airship be used for a trip around Germany carrying leading military figures and Nazi party officials. There was some rush in servicing the Hindenburg, and she experienced engine troubles

on her next trip, the regular flight to Rio de Janeiro at the end of March.

However, these problems were soon corrected and the Hindenburg was declared fit. She was booked to capacity for the first flight of the year to Lakehurst. On the evening of May 3, 1937, she left on the first of 18 scheduled voyages for the year. The sea-crossing took only 16 hours—surprisingly fast, even from the standpoint of present-day air transport.

At Lakehurst Naval Air Station where the Hindenburg was expected to arrive at about 8am on May 6, 1937, the usual crowd of staff reporters, newsreel cameramen and radio interviewers gathered in leisurely fashion. The arrival of the Hindenburg was so routine that it simply received 'society' coverage when a well-known figure was aboard. Consequently, the facilities for news coverage at Lakehurst were rudimentary,

with just one telephone set aside for the pressmen's use.

The crowd of relatives and sightseers were getting a little impatient. German efficiency for once was thwarted, because the airship was late. Captain Max Pruss had sent a radio message in the afternoon announcing his intention to circle for a while as he could see storm clouds brewing up. It rained quite hard about 4pm, but by early evening the weather improved slightly, with only a light drizzle and mild wind blowing. The landing crew, consisting of 110 navy men and 138 civilians, bustled around the mooring mast and customs facilities, expecting the airship to cruise over at any moment.

Around 7pm the Hindenburg glided in towards her berth at the mooring mast. She was a truly amazing sight, a great shining silver-grey object, shaped like a bomb, with steerage fins sloping up

Previous page Press photographers at the airfield caught unique historical records of the Hindenburg in flames.

at the rear, top and bottom.

At 7.19 the Captain gave the order for the water ballast to be dropped, and for the gasbag valves to be closed. The Hindenburg dropped to about 200 feet, hanging in the wind and slowly edging up to the mooring mast. Then the engines were reversed to prevent the airship overshooting her mark or moving in too fast. The whole operation was proceeding in the routine clock-work manner that had created the great Zeppelin reputation. At 7.21 the landing ropes were lowered and some of the ground crew set about hauling them in. Then the steel mooring cable appeared from the nose of the ship, and more crewmen looked up expectantly, ready to winch the ship to her resting place.

One reporter, Herb Rau of the *Standard News*, had already turned his back on the airship, heading towards the one telephone so that he could be first to get in his story that the Hindenburg had arrived safely.

The passengers were clearly visible to the people standing below. The ship was only 75 feet above the ground. Relatives were waving at the faces peering out of the promenade deck windows, when suddenly they saw an awe-inspiring flash of fire burst out on the top of the ship. Mouths went dry. The Hindenburg, the safest airship in the world, was going up in flames.

One of the most historic moments in aeronautical history was captured for all the world to see and hear by that crowd of news reporters standing below. Herbert Morrison, an announcer with Station WLS, Chicago, was blithely filling his listeners in when suddenly his tone changed to near-hysteria. 'Its broken into flames. It's flashing—flashing! It's flashing terribly! It's bursting into flames and falling on the mooring mast!'

Below left The Hindenburg cruises over Manhattan on her last flight.
Below right The stern sinks to the ground, ablaze. The Captain's quick thinking allowed a few people to escape.

Someone shouted 'Run!' and the ground crew, the families, friends and reporters began an almost machine-like movement to get out of the way. This must have been the moment of truth for the Hindenburg's passengers, for inside the airship, most people had only felt a slight thud and passed it off as part of the mooring manoeuvres. Even Captain Pruss had no knowledge of the fire at this stage. A mechanic, George Haupt, saw the fire in gas cell number 4 in the stern of the ship: he gave the alarm and Pruss was contacted by the radio officer who gave him the news.

It was good timing, for when the Hindenburg began to slide out of level, Captain Pruss made a decision that gave a chance of survival to a few passengers and crew. Instead of pulling the blazing airship up to horizontal, he let the stern sink to the ground so some people could jump out.

Bodies were thrown about like beads in a box. Horrified eye witnesses saw small figures, outlined black against the orange glare of the spreading fire, plummeting to the ground. Herbert Morrison was still shouting into his microphone: 'This is terrible! This is one of the worst catastrophes in the world. Oh the humanity and all the passengers! I told you, it's a mass of smoking wreckage, Honest, I can hardly breathe'. He had to stop, as the scene was too shocking for him to be able to continue.

The flames spread first towards the stern, as this part fell to the earth, then leaped along the length of the airship to the front, sticking high up in the air, outlined in a lurid glow. In a matter of moments the whole ship was a mass of flames, and the great Hindenburg crashed to the ground.

Some newsreelmen stood gaping, so shocked that they held their cameras pointing at the ground for quite some time before they came to their professional senses and grabbed at equipment to start filming. One photographer, Murray Becker of Associated Press, was among the few who managed to function and made an historic collection of pictures, the first to reach New York. He described the scene as 'a moment of spectacular madness'. Later in the night, when the disaster was over, he collapsed and cried, looking at the wreck.

Less than half the people inside the Hindenburg survived. Its structure, with 600,000 square feet of fabric and its highly inflammable gasbags meant that the airship was totally destroyed in just over half a minute. Some passengers on the promenade deck smashed windows and hurled themselves out as the airship slid to the earth. Many who managed to get out were crushed by falling metal or burned by the flames before they could clear the wreckage. As the ship fell, it gave a bounce, shooting up again to 100 feet. Some people on the port side mistimed their jumps and fell to their deaths before the ship came down to a safer height once more. One man who dropped on to the wet sand of the landing area escaped the burning wreckage by virtually tunnelling a channel through the ground. Others trying to scramble out of the way found their feet sinking, sucked into the wet surface. A few, with no recollection of how they got out, may simply have been blown clear by the explosion.

Among the last to think of escape were the veteran officers of the Hindenburg: Captain Pruss, Ernst Lehmann (who had taken the Hindenburg on her maiden voyage to South America) and six other senior crewmen. They got out only when the airship came to her final rest on the ground. Max Pruss even then refused to get clear but ran around the burning wreck trying to find passengers and help them to escape. Eventually he had to be physically restrained by three American sailors and was led away, still protesting, with the entire back of his uniform burned away.

The final number of dead was 36: 22 crew, 13 passengers, and one ground crew who failed to run clear of the falling ship. Those who survived were given immediate medical attention by nurses and doctors summoned to Lakehurst by the radio coverage of the event. Most on-the-spot treatment consisted of first aid for burns, some of appalling severity, and administration of morphine to deaden the pain. But many people were so deeply shocked that they felt nothing, even in the most frightful condition. One or two people were able to talk quite calmly and rationally for a few moments, as if safe and fit, before death overtook them, so bad were their burns. After first aid treatment, the injured were taken to hospitals in the vicinity.

Among those who clearly would not live long was the senior Captain of the Zeppelin, Ernst Lehmann. An immediate concern of the officials at Lakehurst was to establish the cause of the accident, and it was therefore vital that Lehmann and any other experienced crew member should reveal what they could about the moments before the fire. The commandant of the Lakehurst station, Charles Rosendahl, put a guard watch on the wreck, so that it could be properly investigated without any clues being disturbed or looted. Then he went to visit Lehmann. The only suggestion that the ex-captain could make was 'lightning'; he could give no other explanation for the airship's sudden destruction.

Dr Hugo Eckener, head of the Zeppelin Company, had other ideas. He got the news in the middle of the night when a reporter from the New York Times rang to tell him the whole story. His first reaction was 'sabotage' but when he made this view public he was forced by his own government to retract it. At the time it would have been awkward politically for the Nazi government to be somehow involved in this major international disaster.

It was not the first time that Eckener had had difficulties with the Nazis. At the start, he had tactfully suggested that his new airship might be named after Adolph Hitler. But the deeply superstitious Führer refused the honour, not wishing to have his name linked with anything that might go badly. If the airship were to crash, said Hitler, it would appear to all the world as a bad omen.

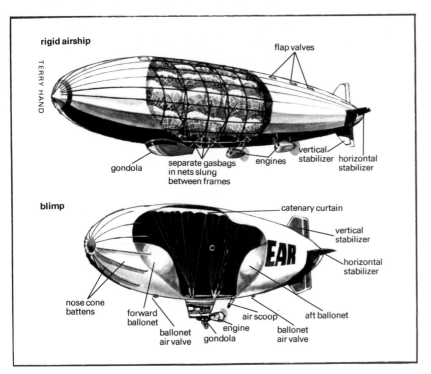

rigid airship

TERRY HAND

flap valves

gondola

separate gasbags
in nets slung
between frames

engines

vertical
stabilizer

horizontal
stabilizer

blimp

catenary curtain

vertical
stabilizer

EAR

horizontal
stabilizer

nose cone
battens

forward
ballonet

ballonet
air valve

engine
gondola

air scoop

ballonet
air valve

aft ballonet

Above *Comparison of a
rigid airship and a blimp.
The ship has a steel frame
and usually carries
hydrogen-filled bags; the
blimp is filled with helium
and uses air compression to
bring it back down to land.*

Instead, the new transatlantic airship was named
after one of Germany's leading statesmen, President Paul von Hindenburg, who had died on
August 2, 1934.

Forced to abandon the theory of sabotage, the
experts, including Eckener, had to fall back on
the 'lightning' suggestion. There was testimony
at the official enquiry from members of the crew,
that fire was clearly seen inside the craft before
she went up in flames. But the enquiry overcame
the conflicting evidence and concluded that
hydrogen had leaked from one of the gasbags and,
mixed with air, had ignited, probably due to
electrical 'brush' discharge, commonly called 'St
Elmo's fire'.

Hugo Eckener later gave support to this finding.
Some of the crew had given evidence at the
enquiry that the ship was handling 'stern-heavy'
at the time, suggesting that a gasbag in the stern
had indeed sprung a leak. 'Escaping gas would
rise and fill the space inside the upper fin and
beneath the outer cover', he wrote later. 'It
would be set afire by an electrical discharge and at
first would burn slowly until the fire reached the
spot where the gas, streaming upwards, was being
mixed with air to form an explosive mixture. This
would produce an oxyhydrogen explosion which
would instantly set fire to the gas within the
damaged cell.'

Not everyone in Germany was happy with the
scientific explanation. Anger was aroused by the
recollection that the airship company had originally wanted helium, a light but less dangerous gas
than hydrogen, for the buoyancy gasbags. But
helium could only be acquired from the USA,
who were reluctant to supply it to the Germans
with the Nazi party growing daily more war-
minded. Finally in March 1938, the American
Secretary of the Interior forbade further export
of helium, effectively ending hope of further air-

ship development by the Germans.

Captain Max Pruss survived his terrible injuries and returned to Germany to campaign for
the continuance of airship design and building.
But the Hindenburg had been too big a disaster,
too exposed to the gaze of the world, and besides
the Nazis were more interested in heavier-than-
air development—for their fighter planes.

Pruss argued persistently with Göering, head
of aviation and creator of the Luftwaffe. But the
latter got his way. That other highly successful
airship, the Graf Zeppelin (both the old and the
new model of the same name), were reduced to
scrap—probably for Luftwaffe planes.

The destruction of the Hindenburg signalled
the end of the airship era. Never again were they
used for long-distance passenger travel. While the
R101 had been a major setback to British development, the Hindenburg struck the final note on a
world-wide basis, largely due to the massive and
immediate news coverage of the event.

Herbert Morrison recovered himself suffi-
ciently to continue his running commentary of
the disaster, interviewing those survivors who
spoke English during the hectic evening hours
that followed the crash. By 12 o'clock next day
news theatres in New York were playing the newsreel film of the Hindenburg to packed houses—
often accompanied by screaming and fainting in
the audience. At 4.30 that afternoon, NBC
repeated Herbert Morrison's entire broadcast for
the whole nation. On May 11, 10,000 people
crowded the New York dockside at Pier 86 where
28 European victims were taken back home
aboard the SS *Hamburg*, amidst a formal Nazi
ceremony.

Ironically, airships were to prove most useful
in World War II against the Germans. The
Americans concentrated on smaller non-rigid
models known as 'blimps' and built up 14 fleet
squadrons which specialized in submarine patrol
and convoy escort work. The blimps had a
moderate speed and a low flight path, so they
could scan the water for submarines and spot
minefields in the distance. At the peak of operations they covered 3,000,000 square miles of the
Atlantic, Pacific and Mediterranean oceans and
escorted 89,000 surface vessels without losing one.
They scored a particular success in the straits of
Gibraltar where they hung in the air and set up a
magnetic barrier, so German U-boats could be
detected and destroyed. After losing three submarines in quick succession, the Germans gave
up the passage. Although lighter-than-air craft
had proved disastrous in the field of passenger
transport, in war 87 per cent were in operational
readiness at all times, a record level of efficiency
and reliability among all kinds of military aircraft.

After World War II Captain Max Pruss formed
a committee to bring airships back into domestic
use, but today they are only used for certain
weather research projects and as oceanographic
research vessels. The idea of airship transport—
for goods, not people—is revived from time to
time, and their chequered career is still continuing.

November 28, 1942
The Cocoanut Grove fire

Below *The burnt-out shell of the Cocoanut Grove, one of Boston's most popular nightclubs in the early 1940s. Over four hundred and fifty people died in the blaze.*

The evening of November 28, 1942, was more than usually festive in Boston's night club district. Alongside the jostling soldiers and sailors on leave from the war fronts in Europe were a great crowd of out-of-towners drawn by a major football game between Boston and Holy Cross. The score, Holy Cross 55, Boston 12, was a big upset; perhaps there was more than average excitement in the post-game celebrations.

The Cocoanut Grove was one of Boston's brightest clubs. It had been open for 15 years, but the sudden increase in clientele, mostly soldiers on leave, had shot the club into publicity and popularity. It had two levels inside, the upper one holding a revolving stage on which the 'floorshow' took place. Downstairs was the newly-decorated 'Melody Lounge' with simulated leather lining on the walls, fancy artificial palm trees scattered among the tables, and swathes of bright coloured silk looped from the ceiling.

That night around 10pm, the club was jammed to capacity with between 800 to 1000 people. Bandleader Mickey Alpert was just striking up the 'Star Spangled Banner' to announce the beginning of the floor show. Backstage, performers were powdering their noses, straightening their seams and fluffing up their curls. Downstairs in the Melody Lounge, a customer decided

to make things a little cosier in his corner of the bar and removed a light bulb from its socket. The barman sent over his young waiter, a high-school boy named Stephen Tomaszewski, to replace the light. Stephen had only been in the place three weekends, making extra money for his family. In fact, his employment was illegal; he was under-age for working at night. He climbed on a chair and lit a match to see what he was doing. After-wards he said he remembered putting it out. Pos-sibly he did but at that moment, a sudden spurt of flame shot across the bar from one of the decorative palm trees nearby.

In only a matter of seconds the Cocoanut Grove was a scene of total uproar and panic. Flames spread rapidly. Hungry tongues of fire licked at the palm leaves, the silk drapes and the plastic upholstery. The mock leather walls began to give off clouds of dense black smoke, stinging eyes and gagging throats. Pandemonium broke loose.

The only visible entrance was the revolving door at the front of the Melody Lounge six or seven feet wide. The front windows on either side were divided into small sections lined with metal. Only the tiniest person had a chance to get through. The doorway was soon jammed with screaming people. There was another exit from the Lounge, but nobody knew about it. Up some steps through an office, a side door led to Pied-mont Street, where the main entrance to the Cocoanut Grove stood. But inside, people could see only blank walls. At the back, the club faced on to Shawmut Avenue but there all the windows had been boarded up to block out the light. The Cocoanut Grove was a smoke-filled inferno trap-ping hundreds of terrified human beings.

As people ran for the door, they beat at their hair, their clothes, their faces, as flames fell from the tatters of silk overhead and set those below alight. Anyone heading for the door could be knocked flat or kicked aside in the great stampede. One man headed blindly towards the back of the club, facing Shawmut Avenue. Mr John Gill from Arlington grabbed his wife and used his free arm to ward off the surge of bodies about him.

'One moment I was moving towards that sound of glass, dragging Margaret with me. The next few seconds or minutes, I couldn't say which, are blanks in my memory. I don't remember that we were borne through that little door but we must have been. I don't know whether we were shoved through or whether we crawled.'

There *were* exit doors in the club. Four led to Piedmont Street, four to Shawmut Avenue, and one to Broadway along the side. But like Mr Gill, no one seemed to see any doors or other means of escape, except the few lucky ones, who got out more by accident than good judgement.

Panic inside the night club was of violent pro-portions. One naval officer who tried to keep calm among people rushing to the revolving door had the uniform ripped off his back. He was found later, slumped among the over-turned tables and

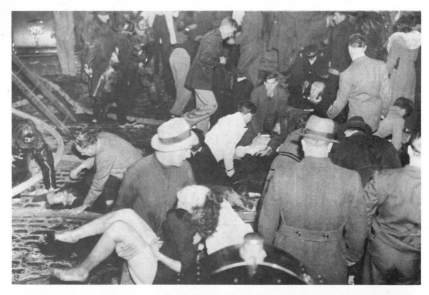

the broken glass, dead.

Some people were so terrified that they screwed themselves into the windows at the back on Shawmut Avenue, having torn off part of the boarding. They got caught on the glass. When rescuers arrived, several had to be cut loose with oxy-acetylene blow torches. Some died where they hung, half in, half out of the blazing building.

A group of the floorshow performers got out to safety due to the quick thinking of one of the chorus boys, Marshall Cook. They were just on the way down some stairs leading from their dressing rooms to the stage when they found their path blocked by a sheet of flame. Cook grabbed one of the girls and swiftly pushed everyone, 35 in all, back up the stairs and out on to the roof. (The building only had two storeys.) There, he found a ladder, which he and some of the other boys held so that the girls could climb down over the side to within a safe jumping distance of the ground.

Several other people rushed down to the base-ment, hoping to find another way out. As the crowd going down got bigger, someone yelled,

Top Victims from the fire are given immediate first aid by firemen and volunteers.
***Bottom** Bodies of the many people trapped inside are removed. Service men on leave were quick to answer the call for help.*

69

'We can't get out this way.' So everyone struggled in the dark to turn and fight towards another exit. A few escaped by locking themselves into a refrigerator room. Some others found a window at the back of the basement, smashed the glass and crawled through.

The fire roared unchecked. Suddenly part of the floor of the Melody Lounge gave way and many people fell through to the basement. By now, flames and smoke were so intense that most people inside the building were dying of asphyxiation, not burns.

The firemen arrived within a few minutes of the first report at 10.15pm and had the blaze under control within an hour. But when they managed to get the revolving door down, a ghastly sight met their eyes. Bodies were piled up six deep behind it. A door next to the main one had a special 'panic lock' that was supposed to release with pressure, but it had been bolted shut. Of the 800 customers in the club when the fire broke out, 433 died inside in the flames, though many more were added to the list later that night and the following day when their burns proved too severe for treatment.

The firemen worked until 6 in the morning removing the dead and injured. Several volunteers came forward to help in the grim task. A passing motorist, Joseph L Lord, a Navy man and a former fireman, grabbed a tool from a nearby vehicle and smashed a window, through which he clambered and pushed out five women. They were caught in the arms of waiting firemen. Mr Lord was overcome with shock at one stage, but after treatment at a nearby hospital, returned to help remove 46 bodies.

Civil Defence workers were called in to help maintain order and give on-the-spot first aid. The Red Cross sent 500 people from Boston and New York with special drugs for burn treatment. So great were the numbers of casualties pouring into the city hospitals that blood plasma had to be released from the city's war-preparedness stores. When nurses arrived to supervize the removal of the injured, they found many wandering around dazedly, while others were completely hysterical. One nurse knocked down two uncontrollable survivors with jiu jitsu.

In the city's hospitals, the dead lined the corridors. No move could be made to identify and list casualties until well into the following day.

William Reilly, Boston's Fire Commissioner, made an on-the-spot assessment of the fire at 2am, once the firemen had it under control. The holocaust had resulted in large part from panic. If people had kept their heads, it could have been possible to control the blaze and get everyone out. Instead 484 people, half the number of patrons in the club, were believed dead, although a later report reduced the death total to 474.

Next day the Mayor of Boston recalled that he had repeatedly warned people about the possibilities of war disasters: 'At every opportunity I have been urging the people of this city to be calm and quiet, cool and collected, in the event of an emergency'. His pleas had gone unheeded.

Perhaps the war atmosphere contributed to the low resistance of that nightclub crowd to the onslaught of terror and panic. The city's civil defence organization had a sad and timely dress rehearsal for possible war events, such as air attacks, in the work of identifying the dead and controlling the crowds who gathered all night and next day around the Cocoanut Grove. At one stage in the night martial law had to be proclaimed in the Cocoanut Grove area.

But it soon emerged that the behaviour of the Cocoanut Grove customers was not by any means the sole explanation for the disaster. The City Commissioner for Buildings revealed that there were neither proper regulations covering the use of decorations in night clubs nor legal requirements about the installing of sprinkler systems and siting of emergency exits. Robert Moulton, head of the National Fire Protection Association, said that part of the blame must rest on 'the chaotic condition of Boston's building laws, incompetent enforcement, political influence and careless management'.

In the months that followed, recriminations spread as wildly as the fire itself had. An immediate inspection of all other night clubs in the city took place, and there was a quick and complete overhaul of the relevant laws. A detailed enquiry was set up and finalized its report in November 1943. It recorded the cause of the fire as 'unknown', but noted that the club had been 'overcrowded beyond capacity'. It concluded that loss of life would have been much lower if exits had been accessible and clearly marked.

A spate of charges were levelled against officials concerned, though few ended in prison sentences. City Building Commissioner Mooney was indicted for failure to enforce building regulations; Captain J Bucigross, a senior police officer, for failure to enforce the fire regulations, and various builders and decorators were accused of supplying substandard materials. One of the club operators, Barnett Welansky, was found guilty of recklessly operating the night club, failing to provide sufficient fire equipment and neglecting fire hazards. He was imprisoned for 12 to 15 years.

Welansky was an easily identifiable target. Bucigross was later acquitted, although the Suffolk County Grand Jury held that there had been 'shifting of responsibility and a tendency by various officials in different important departments to rely too much on their subordinates without exercising sufficient and proper check'.

That was the real source of the disaster, as it so often is with man-made ones. Situations are allowed to slide, to drift, to get out of hand, until a major mistake shows up a failure or corruption of an organization. This disaster may have been heightened in its seriousness by the almost abnormal reaction of the crowd, but in wartime, even greater care should have been exercised by those who had the morale-building entertainment, the comfort and the safety of the general public in their charge.

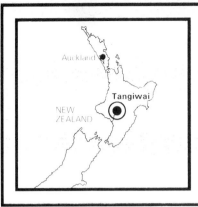

December 24, 1953
Train crash at Tangiwai

Tangiwai is a spot between Auckland and Wellington, New Zealand, where a railway bridge crosses over the Whangaehu River. Its name is Maori, 'Wailing Waters'—appropriate in the light of its history for disasters.

On Christmas Eve, 1953, the postmaster at a small nearby railway town, Cyril Ellis, thought the river looked dangerously high. Heavy rains had been falling for several days, but did not account for the turbulence of water he saw that evening. By some intuition he went to investigate the bridge, which by 10.21pm was already under water. Mr Ellis suddenly remembered the oncoming Main Trunk Express. As it approached Auckland it would be travelling at full speed, and with the force of the water rising as it appeared to be, the train would be in great danger. He began to run along the railway track, in the path of the advancing train, whose engine and lights were just visible in the distance. He waved frantically at the driver. He said afterwards, 'I am sure the driver and fireman saw my signals but they just did not have enough distance in which to stop the train'. With an appalling screech of metal on metal, the train began to slide over the bridge. When it was halfway across, the railway bridge gave way under the weight of the water flooding down the Whangaehu, and the engine, moving at

Below The tangled remains of the Auckland express lie in the bed of the Whangaehu River. The railway bridge was washed away by flood water.

a speed of about 40 to 50mph, careered over the side of the destroyed bridge, taking with it the tender and the first five carriages. The sixth carriage rocked and hovered on the brink, the rest remained on the bank.

There was a rush among the passengers in the sixth compartment to clamber back to the end of the train to safety before their carriage went the way of the first five, but before they could manage it, the coupling linking them to the rest of the train snapped, and the sixth carriage plunged downward into the foaming water. It rolled, floated, buffeted about until it came to rest on a bank of the river about 30 yards from the bridge. The other five carriages also floated way. Most of those who died were in these first carriages. Most survivors were in the three carriages that remained on the bank. Of 285 passengers, 131 lost their lives, and 20 remain unaccounted for.

The lucky ones escaped due to acts of remarkable bravery. Mr Ellis struggled with the occupants of that sixth carriage on the mud bank. As it rolled, one recalled, they were 'floating around, touching people, grabbing at things, but not seeming to get anywhere'. Mr Ellis broke a window in the carriage and with two passengers, John Holman and E J Hartwell, helped to pull people out on to the side of the carriage that remained above the swirling, ice-laden water. Their position was very precarious, for with every swipe of the rapidly-moving river, the carriage lurched and threatened to topple them into the black and seething water. When the 130-ton KA locomotive hurtled into the river, it pulled behind it an oil-laden tender which sailed through the air, landing on the opposite bank where it broke into pieces. The oil spread on the water, adding danger to the struggling survivors, for anyone caught in it risked being smothered, unable to see which way to turn to safety.

The 26 survivors in the sixth carriage managed to form a human chain back to the bank, and one by one made a perilous journey, just a few yards' distance, to safety. The water was flowing so fast that their great fear was of being swept away. Victims recovered the following day had been hit with such force by the water that their clothes had been stripped from their bodies.

Passengers in the first five carriages were not so lucky. In the one immediately behind the engine, a couple and their two children managed to escape through a broken window and struggled to the bank, covered in mud and oil. Another man in the same carriage was swept half a mile downstream before he got any kind of foothold or handhold and crawled to safety. Another survivor described what it felt like to be trapped inside a carriage as it hurtled into the flood:

'Our car went over and we hit the river. We must have rolled over half a dozen times. Mud and water poured in. The car was washed about 200 yards downriver, then stuck on a sandbank and turned on its side. That's what saved us. I smashed open a window and another chap

smashed one farther down the car. We pulled ourselves up and held our heads up in the air. There was somebody on the bank and he ran to get help. I think that's how they got to us.'

He may have been spotted by another rescuer, A Dewar Bell, who had been standing nearby and managed to catch four men in turn as they swept by him, within a few minutes of the carriages hitting the water. He stood in the stream and clasped at the bodies as they hurtled by, in great danger himself. Finally he clambered back to the bank, where he saw a carriage that lumbered on to the mud. Five people were sitting on it. He jumped on to the carriage and smashed the windows. There were another 20 people inside. He rescued 16 in total before the waters took their toll. The speed and weight of the water was so strong that remnants of carriages were found the following day two and a half miles away. Only heavy metal pieces remained—wooden superstructures were broken up and borne away in the flood.

The exact cause of the disaster was soon discovered. Above the valley of the Whangaehu River stands the icy peak of Mount Ruapehu, one of New Zealand's North Island volcanoes. In its centre lies a vast crater, filled by a beautiful lake. It is from the foothills of Ruapehu that the Whangaehu flows, so the source of the flood water inevitably lay there. After the disaster, four experienced mountaineers climbed up to look at the volcano and found that the surface of the lake was 25 feet lower than its usual recorded level, and its total surface area, once 14 acres, was now only three acres or so. Fresh mud and blue clay six to eight feet deep was found round the edge of the crater, several thousand feet above the surface of the water. Some of the boulders there were still hot.

The volcano had erupted, spewing forth a great stream of water, mud and rock, and this found a pathway down the shallow rut of the Whangaehu riverbed. As the water and mud thundered down the mountain slope, it gathered greater momentum and sucked up large deposits of earth, volcanic ash, boulders, whole trees and hunks of ice. Mount Ruapehu had shown signs of activity in previous years and now broke through its crater walls with this devastating mudflow or *lahar*. The volcano had last erupted in 1945, so there were large deposits of ash readily available, adding weight and substance to the sudden flood of water and mud.

The bridge at Tangiwai was no lightweight, flimsy structure. The force of the lahar is evidenced by the total destruction of five out of the seven spans, two of 44 feet in length, and three of 22 feet, standing on thick concrete piers. One of these, crumpled like a rotten tree, washed up several miles downstream. The river had been increased, in one sudden moment, to 20 feet higher than its usual volume. Next day when the flood had subsided, pathetic evidence of its power could be seen where remnants of clothing hung caught in treetops along the mud-smeared banks.

Rescue operations were mounted within half an hour of the derailment. Some survivors went to a small forestry service camp at Karioi, four miles away. At nearby Waiouru, staff from the military hospital rushed out to the scene to see if they could help the injured, but very few needed serious medical attention. Those who escaped were shocked, bruised, covered with mud and slime, but for the most part, sound in body. Twenty-one people were treated at Waiouru, 12 at Karioi and 12 at another village in the vicinity, Raetihu.

Rescuers continued with the grisly business of recovering bodies from the mud for days. Identification was difficult because clothing, documentation and other personal property was stripped away by the icy water.

Some few individuals had extraordinary escapes. One woman was found 300 yards from the crash, buried up to her neck in mud with only one arm free. Rescuers dug her out, and she was carried, badly injured, to safety. Other people may have scrambled out uninjured and got away from the scene in a state of shock, possibly taking volunteered lifts in passing cars. They never reported their getaway and made the official task of assessing the disaster more difficult. Twenty people therefore remained unaccounted for when the final figures were released the following April.

One of the saddest aspects of the disaster was that the train was probably more crowded than usual, because it was Christmastime, and because Queen Elizabeth and the Duke of Edinburgh were visiting Auckland at the time. They had arrived there on December 23rd, and the Queen was to make her Christmas Day broadcast from the capital. She expressed her sorrow in her message, and the Duke attended the mass funeral held at Wellington shortly after the disaster. Queen Elizabeth also awarded The George Medal to Mr A C Ellis and Mr J W Holman, while two other rescuers, W I Inglis and A D Bell were given the British Empire (Civil Division) Medal.

The Board of Inquiry found no one to blame for the disaster. Mr Ellis had provided evidence of the driver's attempt to stop the train, but natural catastrophe simply overcame human effort. Speaking of the driver and fireman, Mr Ellis added, 'They were the real heroes of the smash. If they had not applied the brakes and sanded the line, more of the carriages would have plunged into the river.'

Strangely, the disaster did not prevent the reconstruction of a new bridge in the same site. The suitability of the train route and the remoteness of risk outweigh the evident hazard. This 1953 disaster was by no means the first. Sudden floods in the Whangaehu are recorded for 1859, 1861, 1863, 1889, 1895 and 1925. The 1861 flood took away a bridge near the mouth of the river—those of 1889 and 1895 are known to have resulted from volcanic eruptions of Mount Ruapehu. 9000 feet high, the icy volcano stands as a permanent reminder that the forces of nature are unpredictable and contemptuous of human life and endeavours.

Above left The cause of the flood was an overflow from the ice-bound crater lake of the volcano Mt Ruapehu. *Middle left* The force of the water was sufficient to demolish an entire steel structure. Five out of the seven steel spans of the bridge were destroyed. *Below* Debris from the train was left stranded 15 feet above the river's usual height, indicating the sudden violence of the flood. Remnants were found for several miles downstream.

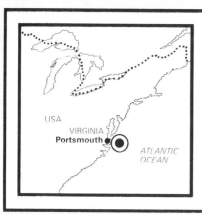

April 10, 1963
Sinking of
USS Thresher

Below USS Thresher, *one of the American Navy's most sophisticated nuclear submarines, was especially designed to reach deeper-than-ever levels in the world's oceans of at least 400 feet.*

When USS *Thresher* was launched in 1961 in Portsmouth, New Hampshire, she was hailed as 'one of the most effective anti-submarine warfare weapons in the Navy arsenal'. Her chosen motto was *Vis Tacita*, 'silent strength'. Two years later her silence brought the world one of its worst deep-sea disasters.

The *Thresher* cost $45 million and was unusual in her design as a nuclear submarine because her four 21-inch torpedo tubes were attached to her conning tower instead of her bow, so that she moved more quickly and easily. She was 279 feet in length and displaced a staggering 4300 tons. Her equipment was so sophisticated that one American admiral described it as:

'a weapons system so advanced in concept and design that no other submarine in the world today can equal her range and fire power for anti-sub weapons. We see the inclusion of a sonar system so sensitive and so powerful that the ocean around her for greater distances than ever before becomes her territory'.

The *Thresher* had already proved her potential when she steamed deeper than any other American submarine a few months before her official launching.

The *Thresher* went back to Portsmouth for some overhaul work in the spring of 1963. Then, at 8am on the morning of April 9, she glided out of the New Hampshire naval dockyard accompanied by her escort vessel, the *Skylark*, for the first of a series of progress tests. The exact nature of these trials was never made clear but two facts could easily be deduced at the time. If the tests were completed satisfactorily, the *Thresher* would be fitted with SUBROC anti-submarine missiles. In all probability, the *Thresher* was going to attempt deeper dives than any previous submarine. The official data released said that depths of about 400 feet were to be reached, and that the first day's test would last roughly six hours.

As this was the first run after the overhaul, 17 civilian personnel from Portsmouth Yard were aboard to make sure that all systems worked well. The Captain, Lt Commander John W Harvey, was an experienced subman. He had been in the

Navy, working on nuclear vessels, for nine years, although the *Thresher* was his first command. He took over just three months before the trials. Altogether, 129 men were on board that day.

The *Thresher* went under at 12.22pm about 30 miles southeast of Portsmouth. She remained in communication with the *Skylark* until 9.17am on April 10, the following day.

The two vessels kept in touch by both voice systems and Morse code, with an underwater hydrophone system. The *Skylark* could follow the sub's course on a sonar tracking device, a specialized radar. The events of the last day of the *Thresher*'s career began around 7.52am, April 10, when the submarine dived down and reported to *Skylark* that it was checking for leaks. This was a perfectly routine procedure. Shortly afterwards, the submarine reported minor difficulties. Then at 9.13am, a message came up that the *Thresher* had tilted, and the crew were trying to right it. Lt James C Watson, the navigation officer and another officer stood in the *Skylark*'s communication room, listening tensely for the next message. Watson reported later, 'There were blowing sounds on the intercom, but nothing else.' The Captain, Lt Commander Stanley Hecker, grabbed the microphone and yelled at the *Thresher*, 'Are you in control? Are you in control?' Twice more he repeated the question. Watson was sure he heard the sub-captain's voice, unhurried, calm, saying, 'Exceeding test depth...' Hecker thought he recalled those words: 'Experiencing minor problems . . . have positive angle . . . attempting to blow.' Then he heard a sound of air rushing into the *Thresher*'s ballast tanks. The next message was garbled. All he could catch distinctly was '. . . test depth . . .'. Put together with Watson's evidence, the facts seemed fairly clear. The world's finest submarine was lying, damaged or unable to move, on the floor of the Atlantic, one and a half miles below. At that depth, water pressure would be 4000 pounds per square inch. The submarine would crumple like waste paper squeezed in a fist.

The *Skylark* tried to reach the submarine through normal communication devices. The probability of disaster was so great that at first everyone must have rejected the idea, trying to convince themselves that the sub had risen again some distance away. But the *Thresher* failed to make its routine report an hour later at 10.17am. The *Skylark* tried Morse code and set off explosive signals every few minutes from 9.17am onwards, and circled round looking for any sign of the submarine's presence.

Finally at 11.04am, Captain Hecker contacted the main submarine base at New London, Connecticutt and reported the *Thresher* missing. Immediately, a massive search operation was set up. Nearby submarine *Seawolf* joined the hunt. Navy destroyer *Warrington* set full speed for the area. Later in the day, this vessel found yellow and red gloves floating on the sea—the sort used in the nuclear reactor section of the *Thresher*. Bits of plastic used as protective shields on reac-

tors were also recovered. These little scraps gave yet more weight to the conclusion that the submarine had broken apart. There was absolutely no prospect of a salvage operation: the lowest depth that any form of rescue could reach was a mere 880 feet, ten times less than the seabed in the area.

The weather grew steadily worse as the afternoon wore on. Forty-five mph winds lashed the search vessels, tossing in deep waves. The sky became cloudy and grey so that spotter airplanes were unable to see anything useful. Visibility was reduced at times to one mile.

Admiral George W Anderson Jr, Chief of Naval Operations, gave the first official statement. 'Very reluctantly I have come to the conclusion that the *Thresher* has indeed been lost.' But the Navy docks at Portsmouth and families and friends of the 129 missing men would not give up. For two days the Navy covered a vast 12,000 square mile area of the Atlantic, its centre at the point where the *Thresher* made its last report to the *Skylark*. On the third day the area was reduced by half. Two frigates, four destroyers, two submarine-rescue vessels and two subs took part in the search. Nothing was found. Not even the wreck of the *Thresher* could be located. A special research craft, the *Trieste*, was shipped from California to take part in the operation. With a special gondola containing cameras and other observation equipment suspended below the main hull, the *Trieste* could go deeper than most other submarines, having achieved a record dive of 35,800 feet. (Eventually the *Trieste* did find the wreck of the *Thresher*, several months later. All that remained was a hulk of twisted metal on the sea bed.)

The official Inquiry set up by the Navy listened to the evidence of the *Skylark*'s officers and took notes from Navy dockyard personnel at Portsmouth. The overhaul work on the *Thresher* completed just before the trials seemed to have been much more difficult than expected. 'We underestimated the scope of the job,' a spokesman admitted. Nor was it the first problem that the *Thresher* had encountered. In June 1962 the sub, berthing at Port Canaveral, was accidentally rammed by a tug. A three-foot gash had been ripped in her hull near the ballast tanks. Even in her first test runs in 1960, deep dive tests could not be completed because 'abnormal strains' were reported in the sub's structure.

The inquiry came to its verdict on June 20, 1963. There must have been a failure in the salt water piping system, so that sea water flooded the engine room. 'The enormous pressure of sea water surrounding the submarine subjected her interior to a violent spray of water and progressive flooding. She came to rest on the ocean floor 8400 feet below the surface.' Much of the inquiry's fact-finding was conducted in secret session, for the *Thresher* was one of the Navy's most highly-prized and advanced war machines.

Why was it so vital that the *Thresher* attempt such deep-sea diving? Although exact figures

Right The US Navy bathysphere, Trieste, *was used in deep-sea searches for the lost submarine.*
Below An underwater camera caught this remarkably clear view of the Thresher's *rudder. The sub lay 8400 feet below the surface of the Atlantic Ocean.*

were never revealed, experts guess that the *Thresher* had been trying to reach a level of about 1000 feet when the accident occurred. An expert in deep-sea diving, Dimitri Ribicoff, said at the time:

> 'If anything at all went wrong, if there was a slight error in her design or if a weld had broken, or if there was any fatigue in the metal, it would have been disastrous. The only reason we don't have more of these accidents is because of good quality control in construction'.

If the hazards are so great, and the technical difficulties so numerous, why is it necessary to do it all all?

If submarines go no lower than 400 feet in the earth's oceans, they are using—and controlling—only 20 per cent of the world's sea. Every attempt to increase depth gives a greater area of possession, power or security, depending on the political standpoint taken. On a more practical level, the deeper human beings can travel, the more convenient it can be, for goods or men. There are no waves to slow down progress and vessels could pass undetected. The *Thresher* was part of a much larger research effort into the possibilities of deep-sea use, especially concerned with acoustics for detecting other vessels. One of the civilians on board at the time she disappeared was the Chief of the Acoustics and Electronics Division of the Naval Ordinance Laboratory in Washington.

The loss of the *Thresher* was a major setback for the US Navy, in military and in personal terms. It stands as the worst incidence of loss of life in the service's history. Only two previous events are comparable. One was the loss of USS *Argonaut* in 1943. She sank with 102 men after losing a sea battle with Japanese forces.

Before that, the *Squalus* submarine had gone down on May 23, 1939, in the same vicinity as the *Thresher*. Water had poured into the vessel's aft section. Five men scrambled into the front of the ship and slammed fast a watertight door, but 33 remained trapped in the water-weighted craft, which settled on the sea bed at a depth of 240 feet. Twenty-six men died in the flooded compartment. There was no choice but to bolt the door on them, for the sake of the remaining crew.

A dramatic rescue operation took place, using a 10-ton diving bell. In groups of seven, sometimes fewer, the survivors were transferred to the bell and brought to the surface. On the last run, bringing up eight men, the lines linking the diving bell to its surface vessel became so tangled that it took four hours to get them straight. All 33 men were rescued over the 48-hour time span from accident to complete recovery.

As a result of the *Thresher* incident, there was a general tightening up of safety testing on all parts used in submarine construction. Twenty-two other vessels of the *Thresher*-type then being built were carefully inspected. The Navy maintained firmly that the basic design was sound. The potential strategic gain is high; risk always accompanies ambitious aims.

October 9, 1963
Overflow of the Vaiont Dam

Below *Two views of the village of Longarone and surrounding countryside, before and after the avalanche of floodwater poured out of the Vaiont Dam.*

The disaster of the Vaiont dam on October 9, 1963, was partly man-made and partly natural. A combination of forces led to the destruction of at least eight villages in the Piave valley and caused the loss of 1189 lives, the greatest number of peacetime casualties in Italy.

The cause of destruction was the collapse of a whole side of Mount Toc, a peak rising 6000 feet above the south side of the Vaiont dam. The landslide fell into the great basin of water inside the dam, forcing a giant wave to tip forward over the front edge, so that it fell almost vertically into the valley 870 feet below. A great torrent, estimated at 200 million cubic metres of water, mud, rock and timber, hurled down the valley and destroyed everything in its path. The dam itself remained intact, although at the time it was thought that such terrible havoc could only have been caused by some break in the structure.

As the wave lunged down across the valley, it hit the bed of the Piave, crossed the river and rushed up against the right bank. Here were situated several outlying settlements—hardly villages even—Longarone, Pirago, Rivalta, Villanova and Faè. Longarone was four-fifths destroyed; the others were completely obliterated.

Nothing survived where the floodwater descended. The Treviso-Calalzo railway line totally vanished: not just the train carriages, but station buildings and water towers were swept away. The tracks were ripped up and carted off. A few miles downstream railway lines were found rolled round and round like giant bed springs. Houses of wood and of stone, electricity pylons, even asphalt road surfaces, were all ripped to pieces by the force of water.

The disaster occurred in the late evening, when nearly all the valley's inhabitants were quiet at home, reading, watching television or asleep in bed. There were practically no survivors. The entire valley was transformed in a few minutes into a vast mud and shingle river bed. Bodies were found lodged high in trees where they had been flung by the violence of the wave. The business of recovering the dead was slow and arduous, and many were not dug out until days later.

The few who survived had tales to tell of their miraculous escapes. A doctor in Longarone, Gianfranco Trevisan, was watching television with his family. His house sat on the northern side of the village, high above the valley, and it survived the avalanche:

'The door suddenly burst open; I called my wife and children and shouted to them to run up the mountain. I thought the dam had burst. We were expecting it . . . Several big landslides had fallen into the lake from Mount Toc. Every so often the ground at Longarone shook, only a fortnight ago the ground shook.'

The doctor's servant was among several house-holders on the slopes of Mount Toc who had been given notice to leave their homes a few days before the disaster. Everyone in the valley had known at once what the cause of the flood wave was.

As enquiries into the cause of the disaster began, it became clear that the Vaiont dam had been a source of worry and fear from its beginning. The dam was constructed from 1956–60 and was considered one of the finest large dams in the world. 261·60 metres high, with a curving wall 190 metres wide, its most unusual feature was the double curved shape of its front wall, like an ancient arrowbow. This design was supposed to give it maximum strength, to resist the pressure of water behind, and at the same time create maximum storage volume, thus saving money. In its thinnest part the lip of the wall was no more than three metres thick. The maximum volume of water it could contain was about 150 million cubic metres, exerting a pressure of 65 kilos per square centimetre. The Vaiont dam was the centrepiece of a chain of five constructions forming the northwest Piave hydro-electric system.

This magnificent feat of engineering was beset with difficulties. Cave-ins and cracks appeared in Mount Toc almost as soon as the dam was finished, causing such concern that the lake was not immediately filled. In 1962, authorization was given by local authorities who had been assured that the dam was a safe structure, although many experts still expressed doubts.

The engineers bored into the mountain several yards deep on either side of the dam and reinforced it with concrete. Special sensitive instruments were positioned on the rockface to record any stress, strain or movement in the rock. A survivor, Rodolfo Barzan, had worked on the dams as a carpenter in the early days and knew of the engineers' worries: 'The technicians knew that part of Mount Toc would fall into the lake. They were waiting for it from one day to the next . . . For this reason they often shone lights at the sheer face of Mount Toc'. He then described what he saw on the evening of the disaster: 'I heard a terrible noise, something between thunder and a salvo from an artillery battery. I thought it must be Toc—the lights on the mountainside went out and a terrible wind began to blow across

Below 1,189 lives were lost in the deluge. The high death toll was due partly to the time of the event: most villagers were at home in bed or watching television when the water hit.

Above *The perimeter wall of the Vaiont Dam, showing the huge landslide that fell into the lake from Mount Toc.*
Far left *Italian soldiers and civilian volunteers help to identify the bodies.*
Left *Part of the Treviso-Calalzo railway line vanished in the flood.*
Right *A few refugees from Longarone leave their partially demolished house carrying a few belongings.*

the lake and then came the wave. Then a thick dusty fog rose everywhere. It was dark and you couldn't see a thing.'

If the thought of an accident was so present in everyone's mind, why did the authorities do so little to warn villagers or to take further preventive measures? It must have been obvious that any break in the dam wall or collapse of the mountains around the artificial lake would result in catastrophe. Only the villagers around the dam lake itself were given any kind of proper notification. The Mayor of Erto put up 'notices of continued danger' in the Pineda district as near before the event as October 8:

> 'Owing to the fact that landslides from Toc could cause dangerous waves on the whole of the lake, everybody but particularly fishermen are warned of the danger of venturing on to the lake shores. The waves could run dozens of metres up the shore, carrying away and drowning even the most expert swimmer.'

One natural phenomenon may have helped to trigger off the Toc landslide of October 9, but it was a final straw rather than the initial cause. There was a minor earthquake in the mountain area just before the face of rock fell. It took place at 10.42; the slide began at 11.15. Seismologists at the Bendandi Observatory at Faenza believe that the strength of the seismic waves showed that strain had been building up inside the mountain for some time.

The force of the landslide changed the landscape of Piave. Not only was the valley floor a massive stretch of mud and rubble, but for a time the Piave River swelled to three times its normal size. Looking back across the desolate scene, survivors saw the wall of the dam still rising sheer and solid, a giant white triangular wedge between two mountain faces. But instead of blue sky above it, a hump of earth, almost a hill, blocked the light. When a helicopter flew over the top of the dam, the pilot saw a new peak rising out of the remains of the lake. At the front edge near the dam wall was a small pool of water; the mountain filled the centre. Only a third of the original lake remained behind the peak. The new mountain had trees still growing, mostly intact, though a few looked a little lopsided, as if there had been a fierce storm. Grass and plants covered the earth between them, and in one place the pilot spotted a small pathway winding up between the trees.

A Government enquiry was set up immediately to find out how such an appalling disaster could have been allowed to happen. Among the many questions which it had to answer was whether sufficient testing and surveying had taken place before the site was selected. One alarming piece of information was the discovery that tests about the suitability of the dam's location were still in progress, three years after it had been completed. The enquiry also had to consider whether the warning notices and partial evacuation of people living around the lake and on Mount Toc should have been taken seriously as an example by the communities living on the valley floor.

When the enquiry published its findings, most of the suspected failing proved to be true. The dam authority, ENEL (the Italian nationalized electrical industry), were found liable for choosing an unsuitable construction site. Various builders and engineers were held equally to blame. Lastly the public authorities in the Piave valley area were criticized for not taking due regard of the dangers and warning their local residents that catastrophe could occur.

May 24, 1964
Lima
Football riot

The riot in Lima football stadium on May 24, 1964, was one of the most bizarre events in sporting history. About 300 people died in the violent fighting and mass hysteria that was produced by a soccer match between Peru and Argentina in the Peruvian capital.

Admittedly, football is a passionate interest among Latin Americans of all classes, but the riot was set against the high tension then running through Peru's political arena as well as the sporting one.

The game was a qualifying match for the Olympic Games scheduled to be held in Tokyo the following year. The Argentine team were in the lead, with the score standing at 1–0. Only two minutes of play remained, when Lobatón, a popular Peruvian winger, scored an equalizing goal. The stadium crowd went wild with delight, but in a matter of seconds their cheers turned to yelps of protest. The referee, R Angel Pazos, a Uruguayan, had disallowed the goal for dangerous play.

The whole stadium was soon in an uproar, and the reaction was so terrifying that Pazos ordered all the players off the field. The game simply could not continue in such an atmosphere, and Pazos was genuinely worried at the inadequacy of police protection for the two teams and himself. They all ran for shelter down a ramp that led out of the stadium.

The riot started. It was triggered off by a well-known football fan, Matias Rojas, nicknamed 'The Bomb.' A thick-set local character, habitué of the stadium, he rushed on to the football pitch to attack the referee. All 40 police and two dogs fell on him and in front of the volatile crowds in the stands, manhandled him and dragged him off. At this, the crowd's indignation could contain itself no longer. With a mighty roar the spectators in the South Stand behind the goal surged forward, leaning and heaving on the iron fence that separated them from the pitch. It gave way, spilling them all over the ground.

The few police on hand had already managed to barricade the players and referee behind the steel door of a locker room, and two hours later they were smuggled out of the city centre.

But innocent members of the football crowd had little chance to get away so easily to safety. Many were trampled to death by the descending crowds. Every window in the stadium was smashed, and fires were lit in the stands—a favoured device of protest among Peruvian football hooligans. The frightened police over-reacted, adding to the pandemonium by lobbing tear gas at the crowd and shooting bullets over their heads. This created panic and a blind flight for the doors, which were all locked. People in front tried to shout, 'There's no way out this way —go back, go back!' but the mob surged forward, forward, so that many at the head were crushed to death or suffocated by the press of bodies. And, the effect of the tear gas on the crowd was acutely painful. One man who rushed up into the stands to get out of the melée felt as if he would choke to death on the gas, so thick was the cloud that arose.

Another man who suffered two broken ribs tried to save his 18-month-old baby daughter by holding her high above the terrified crowd. But he lost his balance and let go of her. She was one of the victims crushed in the crowd against the corrugated iron doors.

The hospitals were soon overloaded with casualties. A temporary morgue was set up, and bodies were laid out on the lawn outside the hospital building where anxious relatives had the agonizing task of wandering about trying to find missing members of their family.

But the events inside the stadium were not enough to exhaust the pent-up emotions of the crowd. Another mob marched on the Presidential palace, tearing down flags from the Plaza San Martin on the way, waving them in the air and shouting 'Justice! Justice!' They wanted to protest to President Fernando Belaunde Terry at the police brutality and to have him intervene officially to have the match declared a draw.

Next day, feelings still ran so high that a third mob stormed the stadium once more, breaking in and stealing trophies and fencing swords from one of the practice rooms. At the university campus a further crowd of chanting students demonstrated, calling for the resignation of the entire cabinet. The student's union called a 24-hour strike.

Out of the crowd of 45,000, at least 300 died and a further 500 were injured. The Government declared a state of emergency throughout Peru and ordered a full investigation of the event. Legislation was rushed through Parliament to give financial assistance to widows and orphans and to pay for the victims' funerals. Seven days of official national mourning was announced.

The funerals began the following day at 9am. Each service was taken individually, unlike the more common practice in other countries of mass burials after such a disaster. The traffic jams created by the mourners stretched for several miles around the main Lima cemetery.

Almost at the same time, the Chamber of Deputies rejected a motion to censure Minister of the Interior Juan Languasco for alleged responsibility for 'police brutality'. And on May 27, the police arrested more than 50 individuals and charged them with looting and incitement to violence. Some had callously robbed victims as they lay dying in the stadium.

A year later, an examining magistrate again called for the trial of the by then out-of-office Minister of the Interior and the chief police officers on duty at the time. In a report submitted to the Peruvian Supreme Court, the magistrate, Dr Benjamin Castaneda, accused them of direct responsibility for the disorders that led to such a severe loss of life. But the Government had given its verdict at the time of the riot: 'left-wing extremists' were to blame for trying to organize

Previous page A policeman with a guard dog looks on as tear gas bombs explode inside the Lima soccer stadium.
Left Spectators scramble higher up the terraces to escape the violence and the fumes.
Above Riot police lob more tear gas in a frantic effort to force the rioting crowds to leave the grounds. At least 300 people were trampled to death.

demonstrations despite the state of siege (a modified form of martial law) that was in effect at the time.

In a report published in the *New York Times* just after the event, American journalist Robert Lipsyte commented, 'In many countries where soccer is one of the few diversions and emotional releases for a poor and restless mass, the game takes on the proportion of a kind of controlled warfare.'

It would be wrong to think that the riot in Peru was a demonstration of a kind of passion found only in Latin countries or poorer nations. There has been a notable increase of violence among sports spectators in many other parts of the world, particularly in England, over the past few years. There were peculiar political tensions in Peru in 1964, but tensions created by lack of money, few job opportunities or mishandled crowd control by the police could cause mass violence anywhere.

Psychological studies on the causes of such hooliganism are beginning to receive long-overdue attention. As yet, no one quite understands how comparatively minor incidents produce such extreme reactions, how the violence builds up or how it can best be controlled. But barricades between the players and the spectators, once a ridiculed feature of South American stadiums, are now being seriously considered for several British football grounds.

Left *Victims laid out in a Lima hospital waiting to be identified.*
Below *The riot continues outside the stadium. Mobs of youths hurl stones at the police. A further mob stormed the stadium the next day.*

October 21, 1966
Landslide
at Aberfan

On October 21, 1966, the people of Aberfan in the Merthyr Valley of Wales were just starting work when a sound like thunder shook the air. At the edge of the village, a rain-soaked, 800-foot-high heap of waste coal slag slipped, engulfing a school, a row of terraced cottages and a farm. The fall ran for half a mile before it slowed down and covered the buildings like a cold, black volcanic eruption.

A local schoolboy watched: 'It uprooted a great tree on its way . . . two other boys ran the other way. It just sucked them away and they ran right into it. It hit the school like a big wave, spattering all over the place and crushing the buildings. It was like a dream and I was very scared.' One hundred and forty-four people died under the tip, 116 of them school children gathered for morning assembly. Ironically, they were due to break up for half-term at noon that day.

'Our strong and unanimous view is that the disaster could and should have been prevented . . . decent men led astray by foolishness or by ignorance or both in combination are responsible for what happened at Aberfan.' That was the verdict of the Government's public enquiry.

Plenty of warning had been given about the likelihood of such a disaster. The tip was over 30 years old, and debris was still being put on top of it when the accident happened. The men working there in broad sunlight saw the tip begin to slide away, but they could not see what happened because a thick fog obscured the valley below. All they could hear was the sound of trees being crushed.

The tip had moved before: in 1959 and again in 1964. In December, 1939, lower down the same valley at Abercynch, nearly 200,000 tons of coal sludge had slid one-third of a mile and diverted the course of the river Taff. Another tip-slide in the Rhondda Valley 40 years before had caused tremendous devastation. Even worse was the disclosure soon after the Aberfan disaster that Mrs Gwyneth Williams had raised the question of safety at a Planning Committee Meeting as far back as 1964: 'We have a lot of trouble from slurry causing flooding. If the tip moves, it could threaten the whole school.' A former head-master, W J Williams, had repeatedly warned authorities and villagers of the possibility. One

of the few 'good' results came about instantly—Lord Robens, Chairman of the Coal Board, ordered an immediate check on 500 other tips in South Wales. The National Coal Board estimated that between 100 and 200 other tips were in a dangerous condition at the time.

An almost willful ignoring of danger signs is one of the basic characteristics of man-made disasters. In the face of overwhelming factual evidence, people seem to say 'It won't ever happen'. No one knows quite why this strange attitude develops. Aberfan has a number of aspects common to all disasters. The work done by rescuers reached heroic proportions in length of hours on the job and fervour of volunteers. When an event of such a terrible nature occurs—and barely a family in Aberfan was spared bereavement—a frenetic energy goes into searching for survivors and struggling to clear up. The body wants to push itself to the extreme of physical exhaustion, so that when the realization of the event hits, it will be too tired, too numb to feel the pain. Shifts at two local collieries were stopped, and miners came up from the coal face, covered in black, to work ten-hour shifts. One man whose daughter was believed dead ran three miles to the school and was still digging at six in the evening.

The compulsion that goes into the work effort sometimes creates inefficiency. At times there were 5000 people digging out the school, the terraced houses, the farm and the streets of Aberfan. People had to be restrained because it was impossible to hear a cry from a trapped person amid the noise of all the activity. As the day progressed, traffic and crowd control became severe problems. Police had to seal off all roads. At first, a Territorial Army Sergeant, Ron McCarthy, who had arrived with a squad of 22 men, volunteered on his own initiative to organize traffic control. From about 5pm, he managed to enforce a one-way system to help keep vehicles moving around the village.

Headquarters were set up in a small room at Merthyr Tydfil police station. Eventually, both army and Automobile Association officials were brought in to deal with the stream of traffic into the village. Ambulances trying to get on to the road between Cardiff and Merthyr Valley found their way blocked by a stream of vehicles carry-

Left Pathway of destruction. Long neglected, the Aberfan tip, 600ft high, had accumulated a vast weight of rainwater. On October 21, 1966, the waste and sludge of the precarious pile slid down on the Welsh village in its shadow, killing 116 children and 28 adults, most of them in the village school, which was completely obliterated by the weight of the slide.

Above left Volunteers fill sandbags to divert the spring water running from the tip and to prevent a further slide from the unstable tip. *Above right* Rescuers work tirelessly, day and night, with flood lighting in the hope of finding one more survivor in the rubble.

ing in pit props, sandbags, shale to make safe temporary roadways, scaffolding materials and cylinders of gas for floodlighting. Men worked round the clock, the whole scene illuminated by the strange white glow of gas lights and the blue flashes of police cars.

Always present was the danger of another fall, because the tip had not only absorbed a large amount of rainwater in the days before, but was also found to have a spring running right under it. Experts measured the flow after the slide and found it was discharging from a single source at the rate of 100,000 gallons per hour.

Coal Board officials claimed that the tip slide was caused naturally by a spring rising up inside the tip. Lord Robens made this announcement three days after the event and was supported by the divisional production director, Geoffrey Morgan, who added that he thought the spring was a recent eruption. Coloured dyes were used to trace the source of the spring and its course. Local people maintained that there was no stream at that site before the tip was started and were more concerned that so few precautions had been taken about the safety of tips in general. This was to be the key issue for the public enquiry.

The problem had started with the onset of mechanical mining in the early 1900s. Coal was extracted from smaller, dirtier seams and vast accumulations of waste came out of the mines with every ton of good coal. Occasionally this slag was taken back down to fill in disused shafts (more in Europe than in the UK) but more often, artificial hills began to burgeon on the landscape. There were complex safety rules for procedures below ground in the mines themselves, but the tips were seen only as eyesores, and responsibility for them was put in the hands of planning committees rather than safety officers. Attempts were made to develop special grass seeds and to bring in suitable shrubs to mask the blots on the horizon, but rules about maximum height were set by planning committees rather than imposed by safety considerations. There were no firm regulations about inspection of tips, geophysical tests or shoring up of sides to prevent slipping.

These were all matters discussed by the Public Enquiry, set up immediately after the Aberfan disaster and headed by Lord Justice Edmund Davies. Born at Mountain Ash only two miles from Aberfan, he had spent many years as a highly respected lawyer in the valleys specializing in mining problems before he rose to the judiciary. He had been involved in the famous Padola murder case and he tried the great train robbers. When the enquiry was set up, the Attorney-General Sir Elwyn Jones issued an order on October 27 that the press and television were to

cease commenting on the Aberfan disaster in any way until the results of the enquiry were published. While many journalists and public figures thought this ban was too strong and infringed the rights of the general public to hear open comment and discussion, it did at least take the public gaze off the devastated village for a while. News reports petered out; the final story dealt with the 10,000 people who attended a mass funeral at Aberfan cemetery for 81 of the children and one mother.

The enquiry proved to be the longest to date in British legal history. It lasted for 76 days, heard the evidence of 136 witnesses and published a detailed report in August 1967. It made absolutely clear where the fault lay and what ought to be done to prevent another such disaster:

'Blame for the disaster rests on the National Coal Board. This blame is shared, though in varying degrees, among the National Coal Board headquarters, the South Western Divisional Board and certain individuals. . . . there was a total absence of tipping policy and this was the basic cause of the disaster. In this respect, however, the National Coal Board were following in the footsteps of their predecessors. They were not guided either by Her Majesty's Inspectorate of Mines and

Quarries or by legislation'.

The report also noted that many of the witnesses had been oblivious to what lay before their eyes. All the danger signs had been ignored, time and time again. 'It did not enter their consciousness,' the report said. 'They were like moles being asked about the habits of birds.'

But the enquiry was at pains to quash the bitter accusations that there had been 'callous indifference' on the part of local Board officials, when people in the village had tried to tell them about their fears of a slide. 'Callousness betokens villainy, and in truth there are no villains in this harrowing story . . . the Aberfan disaster is a terrifying tale of bungling ineptitude by many men charged with tasks for which they were totally unfitted, a failure to heed clear warnings, and a total lack of direction from above'.

One fact emerged from the report which defies belief. It was clearly established that there was no record of any inspector visiting the Aberfan tip for four years previous to the disaster, although this was regarded as part of the regular duty of a mines inspector. No reasonable explanation for this lapse was forthcoming at the enquiry or since.

The report not only laid the blame where the commission felt it belonged, but pointed out

Overleaf *One of the nobler aspects of the various reactions to a disaster is the immense capacity of humans to share hard work and grief. Miners from nearby pits worked ten-hour shifts after their jobs in the efforts to dig bodies from the debris. At times there were as many as 5000 people at work around the site of Pantglas school.*

some basic steps that it felt should be taken immediately. First, tunnels should be built in tips to provide permanent drainage, to remove the danger of another waterlogged slide. Second, the report approved of schemes to re-contour existing tips that could not be removed so they would blend more into the landscape and not be such looming eyesores for the villagers who have to live in their shadow. The enquiry also looked into the European customs of underground stowing of waste, but came to the conclusion that it could not recommend the practice for British mines. The methods used would make mining in the UK uneconomic, and the problems of airborne dust created by the stowing procedure endangered the health of workers on the job.

As to the policy of having tips largely the concern of planning and environment committees, the enquiry made a strong recommendation that tips should be regarded as potentially dangerous engineering structures and that proper steps should be taken to deal with them accordingly.

Although it was felt that a complete overhaul of the National Coal Board would have to result because communications between various levels and departments had obviously failed, the en-

quiry concluded that control of tips should remain with the National Coal Board.

Its recommendation that a National Tip Safety Committee should be set up was quickly put into effect. The Advisory Committee on Tip Safety was established in 1968 by the Minister for Power. The chairman is secretary of the Council of Engineering Institutions and one member is a mining engineer (Director General of Production for the National Coal Board). There are also three Government assessors who work with the Committee, which regularly advises the Secretary of State for Trade and Industry on all matters concerning the stabilty of tips.

The Aberfan disaster produced a number of proposals from other sources. The most important concerned the use or misuse of public money that accumulates at such a time either through voluntary fund raising or the launching of an official appeal.

Public reaction at the time of the Aberfan disaster took several forms, some much less attractive than others. An incredible number of people hampered the rescue effort by gathering into large crowds of spectators. After the event, tourists arrived by the hundred, and police had to check every vehicle in and out of the village to

eliminate non-essential trips. Sightseers continued to turn up, haunting the villagers for many months afterwards. The Queen and Prince Philip, who were deeply concerned and wanted to visit Aberfan, had to delay their arrival until October 29 because of the 'tourist' influx. When they did go, it was one of the most informal encounters ever made by the Royal Family. Local Councillor Jim Williams simply invited the royal visitors to his home, and as they passed through the village, The Queen and Prince Philip were introduced to parents along the way. A wreath was laid in the cemetery; there were no official presentations or processions of cars.

Sympathy and shock were seriously felt by the general public, and a disaster fund launched immediately reached £71,000 by October 26, just five days after the event. (The total sum of the fund was finally closed at £1,606,929 on January 31, 1967.) Princess Margaret launched a special appeal for toys to be sent to the surviving village children and received an overwhelming response from the British public.

But the money and the gifts only created dissension among various groups involved in the disaster. In November, it began to be clear that the villagers would have to battle hard to be properly represented on the disaster fund committee. At first two 'rival' groups arose among them, the Parents' Association of people who had lost children or relatives and the Aberfan Residents Association, representing those not bereaved but concerned about the future life of the village. They soon joined forces under the co-chairmanship of Reverend Kenneth Hayes and Mr Tom Lewis, and eventually got five members on a committee of 15 in January 1967. The general atmosphere of bitterness and frustration about what to do with the money was increased by the strange inertia that set in. Months went by without concrete plans, and no money went to the village it was intended to help. The appointment of a fund administrator in the following May at a salary of £3,000 did little to help; feeling increased that the money was only going to be misused. The pressure for an immediate shareout of the fund gave the world outside a rather misleading impression of the Aberfan villagers as materialistic or self-seeking.

As a result of this embarrassing and painful controversy, Jeremy Thorpe, Liberal MP, introduced a bill in the House of Commons to set up a National Disaster Fund to cope with the understandable public desire to send money at such times of suffering. The function of the fund would be to ensure that a proper amount of money was spent on the right remedies.

The bill was introduced on March 20, 1967, but was not enacted. Another proposal came from Lord Robens, who suggested there should be a permanent disaster force with special vehicles maintained on a regional basis to provide telephone and telecommunication systems and round the clock canteens for the rescue workers. This has not been put into practice either, although a

similar scheme was established in 1974 by Mrs Judith Hart, Minister for Overseas Development, to help cope with foreign disasters.

By far the worst aspect of the Aberfan disaster was the effect it had on the villagers themselves. With all the money, rebuilding and world-wide sympathy, the long-term suffering continues. A psychological study was conducted with the co-operation of the villagers and was published five years after the tragedy. Seventy-three adults and 85 children took psychiatric treatment, although many more who needed it did not go for help. Both children and adults still suffer nightmares; some young ones have experienced such a deep shock and sense of alienation that they make friends with difficulty and dislike going out. The most appalling feature of the villagers' grief was that everyone suffered. There were few to comfort and give strength who were close enough to be of use. So Aberfan turned in on itself. One or two families suffering bereavement can be helped by neighbours and drawn back into ordinary life; at Aberfan the whole village was trapped in loss. The effect on the generation of parents has been worse than for the surviving children, who have more future and fewer memories.

In spite of the sorrow, less than a dozen families chose to move out of the village, and most of those only went to a new estate not far away at Merthyr Tydfil. As often happens when a disaster of this nature occurs, people did not run away but stayed to build life anew. With the disaster fund, Aberfan built a magnificent new community centre, to which the Queen made a promised return visit in March 1973, composed of a concert hall, a swimming pool, squash court, hobbies and games rooms. In Her Majesty's words 'It looks to the future and stands as a symbol of the determination that out of the disaster should come richer and fuller life.'

Above left Immediately after the disaster, the National Coal Board ran a safety check on all other tips in South Wales and found between 100 and 200 were in an unsafe condition.
Above Tips are created from the waste matter that is a by-product of coal mining. In some countries this waste is stowed underground, but this procedure can be a danger to the health of the miners. One result of the tragedy at Aberfan has been better control and regular examination of all tips.
Above right The worst scars of the Aberfan tipslide stay with the survivors. Hardly a family escaped the effects of bereavement.

November 4, 1966
The Florence flood

Senor Piero Bargellini tells a story about the flood that swept through the city where he was mayor on November 4, 1966. A citizen woke early in the morning and looked out of his window at the massive swirl of water filling the streets below. 'I know that Bargellini promised to clean up Florence,' he mutters to himself, 'but I think this is carrying it a little too far.'

That comment is typical of Florence and its people's reaction to the disaster. There is a strong tradition of civic pride and independence, and a general scepticism about the effectiveness of bureaucratic power. The events of the 1966 flood showed all these elements clearly.

Rainfall and flooding in northern Italy that autumn was especially heavy. An annual hazard, these floods caused damage over a 36,000 square mile area. In the 24 hours before Florence was hit, more rain fell in the northeast area than is usually recorded in six months. The valleys of the Po and Arno rivers were the worst affected. Altogether, 112 people died, 11 were reported missing and 5000 families were left homeless. Twelve thousand homes and farms in the countryside and 10,000 houses in towns were destroyed. Hundreds of bridges were swept away. Farm equipment was severely damaged, and industrial areas, especially in the hinterland of Florence, were washed out.

Internationally, the greatest impact was made by the news of the devastation in Florence itself, where centuries-old palaces, crammed with rare works of art, lay defenceless in the path of the River Arno's flood water. In the evening and early morning of November 3 and 4, the river rose 18 feet higher than usual. When the Arno reaches flood level, its two main tributaries, the Mugnone and the Affrico, increase the swell. The first place where the water can gush out over its banks is in the city of Florence. The old part of the town, a cluster of thirteenth and fourteenth-century houses and palaces lies just alongside the river as it runs through the heart of the city. Between the famous churches of Santa Croce and Ognissanti, world famous museums and galleries like the Uffizi, the Museo Bardini, the Museo delle Scienze and the Biblioteca Nazionale stand shoulder to shoulder along river embankments and narrow side streets. Parapets, frescoes, beautiful arched bridges such as the Ponte Vecchio and tiny shops full of Florence leatherwork, gold jewellery and glass complete the most beautiful art centre in the world.

By 2.30 in the morning of November 3, signs of impending disaster could already be seen in the city. Drains were overloaded, with spurts of water shooting up through the gratings in the gutters. The Arno, usually a sluggish stream well down the steep embankments built protectively along its sides, was turning into a boiling surge of dirty water. Cellars along the river banks were already being flooded, yet no official alarm was given. It had been decided by the authorities that too early a warning would cause panic and was unnecessary in any event.

The only people who had any advance news were the goldsmiths and jewellers from the old quarter on the Ponte Vecchio. Some families had been in business there for generations. Loyal nightwatchmen telephoned their employers when the Arno began creeping up the arches of the bridge. Several shopkeepers drove through the torrential rain to save as much of their stock as they could. Afterwards, there was bitterness among the citizens that a few were fortunate enough to be informed, while the majority lost their entire livelihoods.

At about 4am, the full force of the floodwater began to descend on the city. All the morning people worked frantically to move their furniture, vaulable possessions, everything, to the upper storeys of their homes. In the museums and art galleries, a near-hopeless task of rescuing priceless works of art began at dawn. About 7 o'clock, the staff of the Uffizi gallery rushed to work and started carrying oil paintings up from the basement and ground floor. Among works saved were paintings by Filippo Lippi, Masaccio, Giotto, and Botticelli. Over 300 were moved to safety.

In the Museo delle Scienze, the curator, Maria Luisa Bonelli, was all alone. She tried to save the rarest of the museum's pieces, including Galileo's telescope, by carrying them through a second floor window into an adjacent building. The greatest damage to a work of art occurred at Santa Croce, a beautiful thirteenth-century church with a fine cloistered courtyard. In the old refectory, a crucifix painted by Cimabue was torn from its place and thrown into the swirling mud and water. It was 70 percent destroyed, a loss for which no realistic monetary assessment can ever be made. Cimabue was one of the finest late 13th-century painters, a teacher of Giotto and one of the last Byzantine stylists in Italy. Only a handful of his works remain, and the Santa Croce crucifix was considered one of his best. In the Piazza del Duomo, the cathedral square, the famous 'Door of Paradise' belonging to the Baptistery was ravaged by the flood. The two fronts are covered in 20 gilded panels, carved by Lorenzo Ghiberti between 1403 and 1453. Five of these were torn off and hurled about in the filthy water, which at times reached a speed of 80 to 90mph.

All morning, the flood water surged over the banks of the river, over the tops of the oldest bridges, gushing through shop windows, hotels, churches and palaces. Oil drums, dead cows, trees and cars were carried through the town by the force of the flood. As it swirled through basements and cellars, it broke open central heating systems and added the most destructive element to the muddy swirl: oil. Naphtha and other chemicals in the water did irreparable damage to oil paintings, mosaics, delicate ancient frescoes and wall carvings. When the flood eventually receded, a thick black slime of mud and oil clung to the walls as high as the tops of doors.

Apart from works of art, the most serious damage to Italy's heritage was the loss of thousands

Left An old woman wanders bedraggled and forlorn in the mud and receding water of the Florence flood of 1966. A disaster not so much in terms of loss of life but of livelihood, the floods destroyed much of the art heritage which draws tourists from all over the world to the Italian city.

of rare books and manuscripts from the National Library. Monks at Santa Croce saw black, oily lumps floating in the water as it filled the church courtyard almost to the top of the cloister arches. These were rare leather-bound volumes, sodden, stained and falling apart under the impact of the water. 300,000 books were damaged or lost, 24,000 manuscripts, 705,000 letters and other documents and 68,000 musical works. Sadly, many of the books had come from libraries well outside the flood area for restoration and repair in the Florentine workrooms.

Although few people lost their lives in Florence itself, the suffering among the citizens was great, especially as no relief plan or proper rescue facilities materialized until days later. The hospital of San Giovanni di Dio was hit at about 8am. When its basements filled with water, the generator stopped and the hospital soon became freezing cold and sodden. Patients had to be carried up flights of stairs, wrapped in blankets, into crowded, candle-lit wards. At San Salvi, the mental hospital, patients became terrified by the rising water, but nothing could be done to calm them, as the hospital's medicine supply had been ruined in the flood.

In the Santa Teresa prison, panic spread fast, and 80 of the 200 inmates escaped in a mass break-out. Many dived off the roof into the swirling water. Some were recaptured; some went straight to their villages in the countryside to make sure their families were safe. Others were commended for bravery after the disaster for volunteering themselves in rescue efforts. One was recaptured months later in a hillside village outside Florence, where he had been posing as a film producer looking for locations.

In central Florence where the flood did its worst damage, 100,000 citizens were marooned on rooftops without food or adequate protection from the cold. In the late afternoon a lone army helicopter circled over the town, lifting a few to safety.

In the countryside around Florence, help was not so speedy. Many people had been spared the frightening spectacle of the flood because November 4 was a national holiday: Armed Forces Day. Some Florentine families had gone away, so the town was much less crowded than usual. The anger and disbelief of those left behind can be imagined when the national radio network failed to broadcast any news of the flood for most of the day. Instead an endless churn of military marches and high-minded speeches descended on their ears.

By the next morning, November 5, the floodwaters had subsided, and shopkeepers struggled silently through ankle-deep mud to discover the extent of the damage to their little stores. The real disaster for Florence was to its livelihood. Its museums and galleries attract hundreds of thousands of tourists who bring fifty million lira

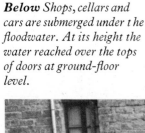

Below *Shops, cellars and cars are submerged under the floodwater. At its height the water reached over the tops of doors at ground-floor level.*

every year to the city. Yet Florence was poor and had no reserves to take proper precautions against such calamities as large-scale flooding. In the late nineteenth century the city had been provisional capital of a newly-unified Italy. Its palaces had been taken over as administrative or public buildings. No money since had ever gone into an organized plan for restoring Florence to its historic splendour. Paintings, books, sculptures and other rare objects were chaotically stored in bad conditions. The flood added to the general disarray which had long existed as a result of governmental indifference.

Military headquarters in Florence were among the first to take effective action. Soldiers were stationed through the two-thirds of the city damaged by the flood to prevent looting or other forms of civil disorder. But for the most part, the citizens moved about responsibly and quietly, trying to restore normality. Priests organized food distribution centres and performed courageous feats, helping to free trapped people and comforting the injured or dying. In the countryside, the Communist party, which has a strong following in Tuscany, set about restoring water supplies and food and acquiring medical necessities. All the local services worked side by side, not always with superb co-ordination from the top, but with great success at local level. Meanwhile government ministers and departments competed in the political game to be the 'single

force that saved Florence' and became hopelessly bogged down in their own rivalry. As a typical example, it was only after six days that the government sent in machinery and engineers to help clear the 60,000 tons of mud and rubble from Florence's streets. Until that time, the city had only 150 pumps to clear buildings of water, and it took a whole day for one pump to empty one basement. Yet four days after the flood, Rome radio announced, 'Florence is returning to normal'. The local newspaper retorted, 'What normality'? Its editor, Enrico Mattei, wrote an open letter to Italy's President, describing the lamentable lack of official help:

'There are some pumps in action, but almost all of them have been brought in from the countryside by private citizens . . . the task of cleaning up the city is virtually at a standstill . . . situations like the one now existing in our city cannot be dealt with by ordinary administrative methods'.

Where central government was tardy, international response was immediate, from experts, officials and ordinary people. Students from all over Europe went to Florence and worked long, unpleasant hours in the museums and libraries, salvaging rare books and helping to save paintings. In the Biblioteca Nazionale, they worked in chains, passing up buckets of mud, and retrieving rare volumes. Sometimes the air was so foetid

Below The Piazza Mentana, Florence. The force of the water swept whole cars, cattle corpses and oil drums through streets.

with the stench of oil and materials rotting in the slime that they had to wear protective gas masks.

Galleries in London—the Tate, the National, and the Courtauld Institute—sent supplies of mulberry paper which is used to restore damaged pages. The young volunteers interleaved the books, which were then rushed to centres all over Italy, to brick-firing kilns, tobacco-curing sheds and other large drying places. An American student described how readily people worked from dawn till dusk, and how the citizens responded: 'The Florentines brought us bread and meat, cheese, brandy, chocolate and wine. You want to give everything to help to the point of sacrifice'.

Various international loan organizations were set up to help the Florence relief work. Between November and the following January, the USA donated $2·5 million in goods, services and cash. A Committee to Rescue Italian Art was set up especially to care for the restoration of the 300,000 books damaged in the Biblioteca Nazionale, while a separate Anglo-American Relief Fund undertook to provide funds so that the small shopkeepers who had suffered could be put back on their feet. Another fund was set up in the UK in November; by December 19 the British had donated nearly £150,000, with a Government grant of £20,000.

The Italian Government at last announced measures to help raise money within the country for the relief of flood-stricken areas. A special 10 per cent increase was added to income tax and greater levies on petrol, cigarettes and alcohol helped to raise the estimated £287 million needed to cover costs. This figure did not include the many long-term improvements that were soon suggested from all sides to prevent a recurrence.

In the welter of public discussion and recrimination that followed, one shining example of mismanagement stood out. Above the city of Florence stands the hydro-electric dam of Levane, 35 miles up-river. It is run by the Italian electricity authority, ENEL (Ente Nazionale Energia Elettrica). On the day before the flooding of Florence, it appeared that the Levane was near its fullest possible capacity. The exceptionally heavy rainfall could not be contained by the dams along the Arno. Higher still, the La Penna dam was already brimming and had let out an unusually large gush of water, which in turn caused difficulties at Levane. Around 9pm on November 3, the gates of Levane were opened and an enormous volume of water was allowed to join the rapidly rising Arno, speeding towards Florence.

ENEL argued that the extra water from the dam was only a minor factor in the rising flood water. The chief blame, they asserted, was due to the increasing flow from the Arno's tributaries. To outsiders such arguments seem peculiar. The authorities in countries like the UK, the USA, Australia or New Zealand measure the maximum volume in a dam or the maximum rise of a main river. But such data is in alarmingly short supply in many other countries, including Italy. ENEL were quoting figures as low as 13 cubic metres

with reference to the dam excess, compared with 250cu.m. from the rivers. But their figures were based on the dam's normal capacity, and no one knows how much extra water it was holding when the gates were opened.

The technicians at the dam did inform the civil engineers that the floodwater was being released, and they notified the police and the prefecture. No one can be sure whether the real significance of the act was made plain, or whether any urgency was communicated. What is clear is that the right message did not get to the right people, and Florence slept peacefully while the Arno swelled up and fell upon it.

Ironically the city's newspaper *La Nazione* carried the news in its early edition about 7am but few people were around to read it, and by the time they were, the copies had been washed away. 'The city is in danger of being flooded', it reported. 'At 5.30 this morning water streamed over the embankments . . . Many families are evacuating their homes . . . there are indications that the day ahead may bring drama unparalleled in the history of the city'.

Along with criticisms of the ENEL and the city authorities for failure to co-ordinate activities and warn the people, many suggestions for disaster prevention soon came forward. The most obvious improvement seemed to be rebuilding the embankments of the Arno to withstand future torrents. More reservoirs were requested to cope with the heavy rainfall that so often threatens the area. The long-term ecological view held that it was important to reverse the policy of tree-felling and indiscriminate grazing on the slopes of the Appenines behind the city. When land is weak, overused and bare, water and soil run off unheeded into streams and tributaries. With reforestation and careful farming, the earth acts like a giant sponge, absorbing a good proportion of heavy rainfall.

However, these remedies were all long range, and the citizens of Florence had a well-founded scepticism as far as the central government's ability to turn plans into actions were concerned. Although Italy is a unified nation, the traditional autonomy of its cities still colours attitudes and actions. In Florence, recovery from the 1966 flood was best made by independent local effort, and government planning from Rome had a limited effect. A leading Italian writer, Nicola Adelfi has explained the problem neatly:

'On the one hand we have a society which is mentally anticipating the future with all the impatience of a man who has just realized that his present home is poky and unhealthy and is determined to move into a modern and comfortable apartment—and on the other we have a national economy that is creaking and archaic'.

In spite of administrative problems, Florence made a speedy recovery from the flood. On December 21, 1966, all the city's museums and galleries re-opened with the exception of Santa Croce. The longer work of restoring went on

Right Self-help was the keynote of Florence's efforts to overcome the ravages of the flood. In the Oltramo quarter, people trapped in their homes receive an ingenious delivery of bread rations and wine.

Left *The Basilica of Santa Croce, site of the worst artistic loss of the Florence flood. A pensive Virgin stands amid the slime and mud left behind. The basilica was under 15ft of water at the flood's crest, but miraculously the frescoes by Giotto in the chapels to the right of the altar suffered only minor damage.*

Above right *Some of the damaged shops on the Ponte Vecchio, Florence's famous old jewellery quarter.*

Below right *Thousands of volunteers, many of them students from all over the world, helped in the salvage operations that followed the floods. 300,000 soiled and broken books were among the priceless treasures eventually restored by these dedicated, and unpaid, workers.*

behind the scenes. The former hothouses at the Pitti Palace were used as headquarters for the operation because it was possible to maintain a moist, even atmosphere there. Water damage causes wood to swell and crack, and if canvas dries too quickly, it shrinks and causes paint to flake. The hothouse solved both problems.

Work still continues on the treasures of Florence: at the time it was estimated that the job would last a decade and cost a minimum of $1–1·2 million. As for the people of Florence, they too made every effort to return to normal. In December, all but 31 of the city's 259 hotels re-opened, and most of those were ready for the tourist season of 1967. Out of the 5000 families made homeless, 500 still had not been rehabilitated by the end of 1966. The leaden Italian bureaucracy tied up public rehousing money for months. One thousand of those offered accommodation were given one room for each family. A hundred or so temporarily took over empty houses in their irritation with the authorities, but slowly these issues were resolved.

Towards the end of the year the government made outright grants of about £287 to small shopkeepers who could prove they had suffered flood damage. In the countryside, all farmers got a lump sum payment of £52, and unemployed labourers received 40p a day until they found jobs. By the end of 1966 all 635 industrial plants in the outlying districts of Florence were once again fully operational. Finally, in December 1966 the government approved a budget of £115 million for rebuilding embankments along the Arno, updating flood warning systems and instituting soil conservation programmes.

August 16, 1969
Hurricane Camille

Hurricane Camille was described as 'the greatest storm of any kind that has ever affected this nation, by any yardstick you measure it' by Dr Robert Simpson of America's National Hurricane Centre.

On August 16, 1969, the sky grew black in the middle of the day. Early warning systems had picked up news of a fearsome 115mph wind that had savaged its way across the province of Pinar del Rio, Cuba, causing serious damage to the island's tobacco and coffee bean plantations. Now it was heading across the Gulf of Mexico, direct for the coast. By 11pm the wind had risen and air pressure was low. Camille tore into Mississippi and Louisiana that night killing 235 and making 200,000 homeless. Both states were declared disaster areas by the government.

The trail of destruction stretched from Florida in the east around the Gulf to New Orleans. The coast suffered most but the immediate area of damage stretched inland five miles. At times the winds were 205mph, with the power to fling three huge tankers on to the foreshore and turn a tugboat upside down. Worst hit were the Mississippi coast towns of Gulfport, Biloxi, Bay St Louis and Pass Christian, where 100 bodies were found of a population of 41,000, and every house suffered damage. Bay St Louis, a lumber milling and fish-packing centre, lost half of its main business street. All the buildings on the east side fell straight into the bay. In Gulfport, 23 bodies were found in one apartment block. Twelve of them had ignored hurricane warnings advising immediate evacuation and gathered instead for a 'hurricane party.' In Biloxi, half a church was ripped away, and not a single house escaped the hurricane. In Gulfport looters and crowds of sightseers fell on the town's wreckage the following day.

Below and right These aerial views show typical hurricane damage. Houses are flattened into a pile of matchsticks in Biloxi, Mississippi, one of the coastal towns worst hit by Camille.

The Governor, John Bell Williams, imposed martial law and ordered a 6pm to 6am curfew to restrict the movements of unauthorized people. National Guardsmen were placed on duty here and in Biloxi to control rioting, looting and gathering crowds.

Louisiana suffered just as badly. Small towns like Buras, Venice, Boothville and Triumph were wiped off the map. The commissioner of Plaquemines Parish, Howard Wilcox, described what was left the next day. 'There are no grocery stores. Nothing, period. A few telephone poles, tugs in the marsh, houses in the marsh—parts of them.' In southeast Louisiana $6 million worth of damage was created in one night.

By late afternoon, August 17, Hurricane Camille was still raging north around Greenwood, Mississippi 300 miles inland, spilling heavy rains and causing massive damage as far away as Virginia, centred on the town of Richmond where 46 people lost their lives.

How can a hurricane wind do so much damage? Air circling around the earth exerts varying degrees of pressure on the surface, measured by a mercurial barometer. Normal atmospheric pressure at sea-level is 29·92 inches. Hot air rises; cool air falls. The amount of moisture in air affects its pressure as well: the greater the amount of water vapour in the air, the lower the pressure falls. Air over the equator rises; cooler air moves in to take its place. The higher levels of low-pressure air move faster than the air caught near the surface of the earth.

All these factors create currents and swirls of air above the earth. A hurricane is a giant mass of rotating air, from 50 to 500 miles in diameter. At the centre of this air-spin are clouds, rain and high-speed winds travelling in a left-right circular motion. As it spins, the hurricane forces air out the top of its funnel and consequently sucks up anything in its path because of its central vacuum. As it passes over land from the ocean, a hurricane picks up speed, sometimes moving forward at the rate of 50mph, although the circular winds inside the storm may swirl at speeds over 100mph. As the hurricane weakens, torrential rain pours out of it. Ironically, in the centre at the 'eye' of the hurricane, there is complete calm and sun may shine through the clouds.

From 1900 to 1969, 12,000 lives were lost in the USA from hurricanes. As can be imagined, the incredible power of a hurricane's circular motion causes the damage, not a high speed forward-moving wind. The storm advances comparatively slowly, giving a chance for people to be evacuated before it hits. In Cuba only one person died, while 15,406 were evacuated. In the USA, 100,000 people went to specially-prepared Red Cross shelters along the Gulf coast to avoid the onslaught of Hurricane Camille.

There are precautions that can be taken by people who live in known hurricane areas. In the Gulf states, luckily, loss of life was reduced by the general awareness of how great the danger could be. Every home should know a planned evacuation route and find out the height of the property above sea-level, for almost as much damage is caused by tidal waves as by the wind. Clean drink-

Below Records from the US National Environmental Satellite Centre in Maryland trace the path of Hurricane Camille for five days, from August 13 to 18, 1969.

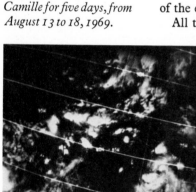

Aug. 13

Aug. 14

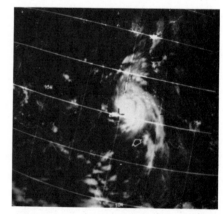

Aug. 15

Aug. 16

Aug. 17

Aug. 18

ing water should be stored in jugs, baths or cans, because municipal supplies may be cut off for days. If possible, cars should be filled with petrol for the same reason. After Hurricane Camille, petrol and water were the main targets for looters and black marketeers. The eye of the hurricane, where everything appears calm, is a treacherous spot to be caught. A lull will last from a few minutes to half an hour. Then suddenly a fierce wind rushes up from the other side of the eye. Excessive rainfall from hurricanes often causes flooding, so rivers and streams should be avoided. In New Orleans, 12 blocks had to be evacuated during the night of August 16 when levees protecting an industrial canal gave way, flooding neighbouring streets with water. But apart from isolated incidents, the city was not badly hit by Camille.

As the hurricane passed north over Virginia, ten inches of rain fell in one torrential downpour, causing 75 deaths and leaving 111 missing. This rainstorm was totally unexpected to both citizens and coastal meteorological experts. It struck Richmond harder than any flood in the city's history. The famous 'Tobacco Row' of warehouses and factories was badly hit, despite preventive measures. Sandbags had been used to block up doors and windows, but the flood water came four feet higher than the dikes protecting the Row. Higher up the James River, swollen to a torrent by Camille's heavy downpour, several small villages were seriously damaged. They had hardly any warning of the James flooding and no time to protect their farms. Property damage in

the state ran to an estimated $18 million.

Within hours of Camille's passing, a massive Federal and State aid programme got under way. A million dollars each was advanced to Louisiana and Mississippi, while the Red Cross raised an appeal fund with a target of £15 million. Sixty-nine thousand families were injured, or made homeless, or both, in two states, West Virginia and Viriginia. By August 22, a fleet of planes, trains and lorries were bringing in food, medical supplies and equipment and thousands of disaster workers arrived. Gulfport's airport was closed to commercial planes and became a distribution base for thousands of pounds of food supplied by neighbouring states such as Georgia. The Illinois Central Railroad of Chicago sent an emergency train on August 21 loaded with relief workers, three water-tank cars, 20 baggage cars of food and an electric-powered generating car. Fort Benning, Georgia, sent a 700-man engineer battalion with a medical force and water-purifying systems that could produce 1500 gallons per hour. Bulldozers, mobile kitchens and temporary homes were supplied by the Army.

The relief effort was the biggest ever staged by America for one disaster. However, not all its operations met with praise and favour. Months later in January 1970, when immediate needs had been met and long-term problems were being encountered, local groups in Mississippi and Louisiana made strong protests to government agencies and the Red Cross about the discriminatory methods being used to help the sufferers. A basic problem was whether to return people to

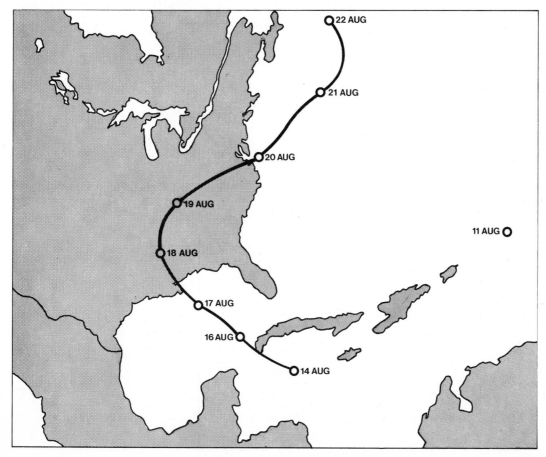

Left Camille began as a small patch of turbulence far out over the Atlantic. As she moved over the Gulf of Mexico she gathered the strength and momentum that eventually made her one of the worst storms ever to hit the coast of the United States mainland.

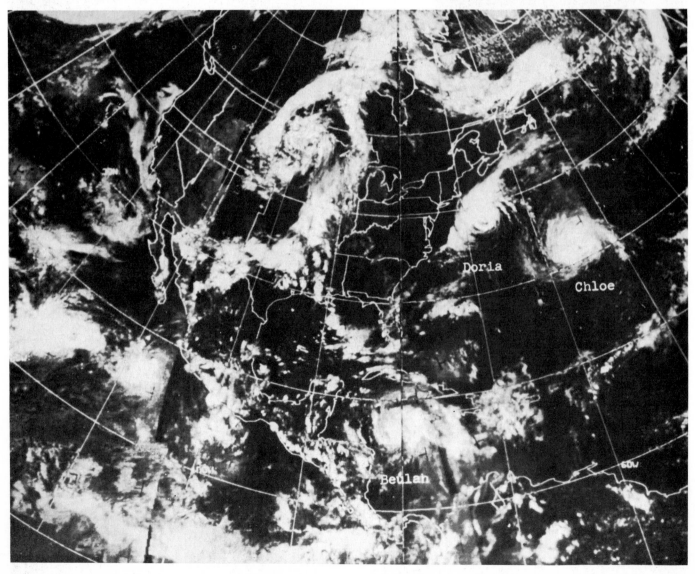

Far left Looking down on the storm, the 'eye' of a hurricane is clearly visible.
Near left A small child is rescued from the floods that occurred in New Orleans after Camille.
Below left Satellite pictures of three hurricanes on September 14, 1967. These early warnings give meteorologists time to warn local inhabitants of storm's approach.
Above right The force of Camille's destructive power obliterated much of the small town of Bay St Louis, Mississippi.
Below Hurricane winds can reach speeds over 100 mph at their peak, lashing the shore with a fierce intensity.

their pre-disaster living conditions or to use the opportunity to give a fresh start to many in dire economic distress. A lack of clear policy led to such actions as giving white families cheques to replace lost clothing, while black families rummaged through piles of secondhand garments. And, white citizens maintained that blacks were getting free handouts from federal agencies. As one American politician put it:

'The question we now face is whether to seize the opportunity presented by a disaster like Camille to correct some past conditions. How far can the Federal government go to rehabilitate a community? That's a concept that hasn't been fully defined.'

This kind of problem can produce bitter debate among the parties involved. A similar situation, though on a lesser scale, occurred in Aberfan, where some citizens wanted to use the disaster fund money to improve the village generally, while others wanted to reserve it for memorials and awards for the bereaved. A disaster magnifies the underlying social ills of an affected community, causing conflict and difficulty for everyone concerned in the relief work.

Hurricane Camille also led to severe criticism of the early warning system operated in the Gulf states. Experts felt that people had been lulled into a false sense of security by regular radio broadcasts, instead of being spurred to action. A better educational programme is needed so that when a hurricane is forecast, people are prepared to act and not to ignore danger signs. Better aircraft and other weather observation methods improve chances of accurate predictions, but at present forecasting can be as much as 100 miles out in 24 hours.

In January 1970 a new data-collecting network was set up by the US Army in five New England states. A pilot scheme, it monitors 35 flood control reservoirs and six hurricane barriers. These 41 sites are linked up automatically so that if telephone lines are knocked down by storm or flood, the system still operates to transmit warning information. Several more such link-ups are planned for other areas of the USA subject to floods or hurricanes.

Camille's nearest rivals in recent US history are Hurricane Beulah, that smashed into Texas in 1967 with a pressure recording of 27·38 inches over the Gulf, though this decreased by the time she got to land. Camille recorded 26·61 inches. Hurricane Carla hit the same state in 1961, with an eye 30 miles across and a trail of damage over 30 miles. By far the worst in this century, though highly localized, was the 1935 Labor Day hurricane, with a recorded pressure of 26·35. It totally destroyed a section of the Florida Keys further to the east. Hurricane Betsy, in 1965, though not so great in force, probably did more physical damage, estimated at around $1·4 billion.

But the physical damage left by a hurricane, severe though it may be, is less worrying than the psychological shock suffered by those people who have felt the storm's force and lived to remember the experience. It may take days, even months, before the victims whose lives have been affected can return to a normal way of life. Indeed, some never do. The loss of a loved one, or of a home where all the memories of a lifetime are stored, can be that devastating.

Below left Storm damage in Massachusetts. With the winds came torrential rain that travelled northeast across the United States, causing floods here and in Virginia.

Below right Hurricane clouds can be clearly seen on any of the radar scopes that form an early-warning network around the Gulf of Mexico and up the Atlantic coast.

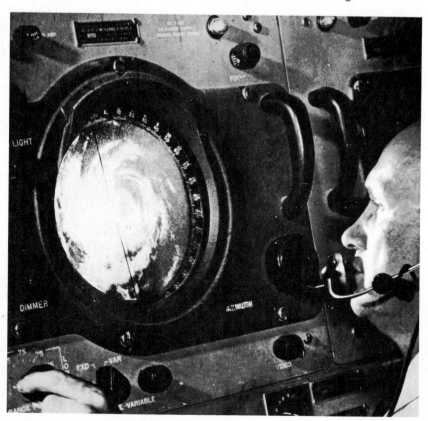

AUSTRALIA

Yarra River

Melbourne

October 15, 1970
Collapse of the
West Gate bridge

About midday on October 15, 1970, most of the workmen on the West Gate bridge project in Melbourne, Australia knocked off for lunch break. They were sitting together in their huts, just below a section of the bridge currently under construction. With no warning, the 1,200 ton part of the bridge came crashing down on top of them. As it fell, it demolished one of the supporting piers which crashed into the mud and sludge of the west bank of the Yarra River.

Some men were still on the job atop the span. They fell with the bridge and were instantly either crushed or burned to death. A few managed surprising escapes and could give vivid descriptions of what happened. Frank Piermarini, an Italian immigrant, was working as a rigger inside the bridge itself, about 160 feet up.

'At first I felt it shaking, but I thought it was my imagination and kept on working. Then the whole damn thing sagged in the middle.

'I could see daylight through the enormous cracks. . . The noise was tremendous. As I tried to scramble out the whole world seemed to go into a massive slide. Everything became black and I thought I was finished. When I came to, I found myself deep in thick oil and slush. There were bodies everywhere'.

Thirty-five workmen lost their lives, including Jack Hindshaw, Resident Engineer for the steelwork designers, and three other engineers.

Within minutes, the alarm was given and relief services rushed to the site. A fire broke out because diesel oil had spilled and ignited, seriously hampering rescue efforts. Injured men were sprawled in mud and oil. Cranes were needed to lift fallen sections of the span off men trapped beneath. Some bodies were not found for several days. Doctors came from the nearby suburbs of Melbourne to give emergency treatment to the injured, and a few Catholic priests moved among the victims giving last

Below *As the west span of the bridge collapsed, Udo Rockman, aged 10, was learning to use his father's camera nearby. He snapped this picture as the massive structure of steel toppled to the river bank below.*

rites to those in need.

Work on the bridge came to a standstill. An enquiry was set up under Mr Justice Barber of the Supreme Court of Victoria. Its work was to prove long and arduous, for the background to the West Gate bridge was a saga of technical problems and human conflict.

It quickly emerged that Hindshaw, the steelwork designers' engineer who died, and his senior assistant had that morning been called to the span that collapsed because a stage in the erection was manifestly going wrong. Hindshaw had telephoned the senior adviser to the contractors, Gerit Hardenberg, to say that he was worried about worsening buckling of the steel plates making up the box-girder. He got so far as to say, without much panic, 'I wonder if I should call the bods off'.

Hardenberg replied, equally without alarm, 'I will come over'. He got into his car and began to drive to the ferry on the east bank. As he got near, he saw the span give way.

The West Gate bridge was intended to be a remarkable feat of bridge construction. It was designed as a cable-stayed box-girder bridge, a method that had been developed since World War II (although a highly successful box-girder bridge had been developed by Robert Stephenson in the nineteenth century, exemplified by his Menai Straits bridge, 1850). The method was acknowledged to be well-suited to places where the width of the total span was between 500 and 1,200 feet. The central span of the West Gate bridge was to be 1,102 feet, the longest of its kind at that time. 'Box-girder' construction is economic and quick and reduces maintenance costs. It combines elegance of line with great strength, which is especially important in long, slender bridges.

The overall length of the West Gate was 8,500 feet, including pre-stressed concrete approach viaducts on either side, supported on slender concrete columns. The main section, between piers 10 and 15, would consist of five steel box-girder spans, the three middle ones partly supported by steel cables stretching from two steel towers on the twelfth and thirteenth piers 150 feet above the roadway. The Lower Yarra Crossing Authority Limited, who were in charge of the project, were pleased with the magnificence of the design and saw it as a beneficial development, linking Fort Melbourne and Williamstown to improve the flow of commercial traffic. The only link before was a ferry at Williamstown, which was proving inadequate as Melbourne expanded.

Freeman Fox and Partners, a distinguished firm of design consultants, were responsible for the steel design, but as is the custom in the field, construction would be in the hands of an independent contractor. Neither would Freeman Fox be involved with the design of the concrete sections, which remained in the hands of the other consultant designers for the crossing, Maunsell and Partners of Melbourne.

The problems seem to have started with the

Below *The huge steel span fell away from the concrete support pillar and landed on the workmen's sheds below, demolishing the flimsy structures and killing a number of the men who were having lunch in their huts at the time.*

centre steel sections. The steelwork contract was first awarded in 1968 to a Dutch firm, World Services and Construction Limited, but they were forced to pull out in 1970. The official enquiry described their failure as 'lack of diligence and failure to make good time', although it also noted that the company had been bedevilled by strikes and bad labour relations from the beginning.

Much time had been lost, and a lot of money sunk in the project. The Lower Yarra Crossing Authority wanted to move ahead with the work as fast as possible. Its next choice was a local firm, John Holland and Company. This firm had successfully built the approach viaducts, but had little experience with bridge-building of this sort. It knew more about concrete than it did about steel, but the Authority felt it was tough and efficient and would get the job done. As the firm had come in at a mid-way stage, World Services were retained to give them technical advice. Freeman Fox acquiesced in the new arrangement, which called for more advice and supervision from them.

The agreement resulted in chaos, with confused responsibilities and inadequate communication between the Crossing Authority, Maunsells, Freeman Fox, World Services, John Holland, and not least the construction workers and their unions. Freeman Fox were not accustomed to such a situation, and the enquiry concluded that 'while we have found it necessary to make some criticism of all the other parties, justice to them requires us to state unequivocally that the greater part of the blame must be attributed to Freeman Fox & Partners'.

The method to be adopted for erecting the girders is crucial in all major bridge designs, and box girders can be built where temporary supports are impractical by a spectacular but tricky process, 'cantilevering out', in which complete sections of sixty feet or so at a time are assembled and slid out along the complete deck to be attached at the end. Four months before the Yarra accident, a box girder had collapsed at Milford Haven in Wales during this cantilevering process, killing four men.

The same method had been successful for Freeman Fox over the Wye Viaduct in Britain, a similar type of cable-stayed box-girder, completed in 1966, and will still be used for the main span at West Gate. For the spans at each end, it was necessary to assemble the complete length of span on the ground and then hoist it into position. To make this procedure easier, only half the width was dealt with at a time, and the two halves therefore had to be stitched together with bolts throughout their length after reaching their intended final position.

When this was attempted, the two halves were discovered to be out of level in the middle

Left *Rescue work began quickly, with fellow workers helping to free trapped and injured men and carry the bodies of the dead away.*

111

by up to four and a half inches and buckling, or wrinkling, of the thin steel plates had occurred. A procedure had been agreed and successfully used to correct the span already built in this way on the east bank. As well as being tricky, this was a complicated and time-consuming procedure for it required hydraulic jacks to be brought in and operated at carefully phased points along the length.

For the corresponding span on the west side, John Holland were eager to use a quicker procedure, with 'kentledge' – they simply laid some 60 tons of concrete blocks to weigh down the higher side. A buckle appeared immediately in the edge of a plate in the loaded span close to mid-span. Because of labour problems little progress was made in stitching the two sections together. On October 15, six weeks after the buckle had appeared and on the instruction of a junior engineer, bolts holding the buckled plate were removed to try and smooth out the buckle. The girders were still supporting their own full sagging weight and removing the bolts greatly increased the stresses at mid-span.

On the site there were failures of communication and a lack of definition about where responsibility lay. The operation of removing bolts to straighten the buckle was in progress when Hindshaw and his assistants were called to the deck on the fateful morning. Hindshaw saw that the buckle had become greatly extended and told the men to replace the bolts, but the buckle got worse, not better. Then he made his last telephone call, just before the span collapsed.

The close sequence of the Yarra and Milford Haven disasters, together with two comparable cases in Europe, led to a major effort on research and to rethinking the current philosophy of ensuring safety in new forms of construction. This included considerable tightening up on systematic checking of designs. The result is that such bridges are now more costly, but considerably less dependent on the most unpredictable aspect of bridge building: the successful cooperation between designers and engineers. It seems less than satisfactory that many details of design and erection procedures should be a matter of day-to-day discussion, or worse, guesswork.

The West Gate bridge is still under construction, with a new consortium on the job. Greatly improved safety margins have been worked into the erection procedures: temporary cables add support until the bridge is completed, and the construction design has been modified to provide extra strength and safety, although the external appearance and original beauty of the bridge will not be lost.

Below *Construction continued as soon as it was possible. This photograph, taken in 1974, shows a half-section about to be floated out to the main structure, where it will be attached along its perpendicular edge to a corresponding half-section to form a complete box.*

St Laurent du Pont

Grenoble

FRANCE

November 1, 1970
The Cinq-Sept fire

The Club Cinq-Sept was the most popular rendezvous for miles around the little town of St Laurent du Pont. Young people in their late teens and early twenties came from Grenoble, 20 miles away, from Aix-les-Bains and Chambery to dance and drink with their friends in the hangar-like building. Surrounded by forests, the Club Cinq-Sept looked very ordinary from the outside —a large plain shell of a structure with a corrugated iron roof. Inside, it was the latest thing in psychedelic decor. Plastic-covered columns created a fantastic grotto effect. The bands played on a small platform downstairs at the back; above

were little alcoves with windows overlooking the dance floor. The only way up was via a spiral staircase.

On Saturday, November 1, 1970, the Club was packed to capacity. A rising new group from Paris called 'Storm' were playing their first date at the Club, and people had come from all over the region to hear them. The main entrance to the Club was through a turnstile, a continental kind that stands seven or eight feet high and has spokes sticking out all the way down. So special was this night that all the other exits had been locked to prevent gatecrashing.

Below The burnt-out interior of the Club Cinq-Sept where 144 young people lost their lives in a matter of minutes.

Around 1.40am, there were still nearly 200 young people in the Club, dancing in a trance to the powerful sounds of 'Storm'. In one of the little alcoves upstairs, a youth dropped a match on to a cushion. Within seconds, flames were shooting up beside him. At first he and his friends tried beating them out with the palms of their hands and their coats and jackets. But the flames seemed to have a will of their own.

Some of the kids upstairs passed the word, 'Fire!' and a number of the ones sitting there went straight down the spiral staircase, across the dance floor and out the front door. As the word was being passed to the people below, a giant flame shot down the length of the dance floor. The band, playing their big finale, the Stones' *Satisfaction*, did not have time to move. No more than 30 seconds after that flash of fire, the entire psychedelic interior of the Cinq-Sept was transformed into a swirling mass of smoke and flame. The plastic arches, like some mad dream of a pit of hell, melted to the ground, dropping burning lumps on to the bodies beneath.

One barman hurled himself against the only available emergency exit at the northeast corner of the building. He and a handful of youngsters standing near him got out that way. Only about 30 escaped through the main turnstile before panic and chaos seized everyone inside. The turnstile jammed, and no one else could move. Afterwards firemen found one boy impaled on the spokes of the gate.

Within a minute of the fire's start, the place was choking with acrid fumes. Some couples were overwhelmed where they stood, found later in each other's arms on the dance floor, by the bar, in corner seats around the walls.

One hundred and forty-four young people died almost instantly in the blaze, including two of the three club owners. The third, Gilbert Bas, 25, had been in his office and saw a warning light flash on the electricity control board. Perhaps there was a fight going on; he rushed to the main hall to see if he could help. As he got near he heard the anguished screams of 'Fire, fire'. Then the greatest of the club's many defects flashed into his mind. There was no telephone. Bas had to get into his car and drive over a kilometre to the fire station, while lives were lost behind him.

The local firemen arrived but there was nothing they could do. As one fireman said, 'They didn't have a chance, the place went up like a matchbox.' It took the firemen all night to get the fire under control. No one could be rescued. At the end, the walls still stood, but the roof had melted away in the heat of the blaze. From 5am until well into Sunday morning, the unpleasant task of extricating the charred bodies went on until the town hall, converted into a temporary morgue, was filled with rows of the dead. The authorities showed tremendous tact in dealing with relatives of the victims. It was decided that night that no one should identify the bodies. Many were too badly burned to be recognizable. Instead, personal belongings that survived—cigarette lighters, watches, jewellery—were placed carefully in small yellow envelopes. Opening these packets was how most parents learned the news next day when they crowded to the scene.

Understandably, the initial reaction to news of the fire disaster was not only shock but anger. An enquiry was set up at once to look into the background to the Cinq-Sept, while on a broader basis, the event led to an immediate investigation of all similar dance halls, discotheques and clubs in the region. One club at Clermont à Oise was closed immediately, a second at Nancy was refused a building permit.

Reactions of shock, anger or apprehension of further danger are, sadly, only part of the typical pattern of post-disaster behaviour. The other common one, morbid curiosity, soon created a massive problem for the town's over-taxed police force. By lunchtime on Sunday all main streets and access roads in St Laurent du Pont were jammed with sightseers. It took 200 men to control the crowds who had no legitimate reason to be there, but who pressed forward around the site of the club, the town hall and elsewhere.

Almost at once certain indisputable facts emerged. In France there are numerous fire and safety regulations that would apply to an enterprise like the Cinq-Sept, the principal ones becoming law in 1965 and 1969, recently enough to be recalled by anyone in authority. First, the local Building Safety department is supposed to visit new premises before they can open to the public. Building permission had been granted to the Cinq-Sept, but a final inspection had not taken place. Second, there are rules which relate the number of people a place can hold to the type of safety precautions required. The rules at the Club were virtually non-existent. Normally there must be two doors besides the main one to be used as exits, in addition to two emergency fire exits. The two access doors can be kept locked legally, but someone with keys must be present whenever the hall is open to the public. At the Cinq-Sept, there was open evidence of flagrant disregard for this safety rule. Of the three access doors required, one was sealed during the building operation. The second was locked at the time of the dance. In addition, the two regulation fire exits were not illuminated. One was hidden by a screen behind the bandstand; the other was in a darkened corner of the dance floor, its access blocked by stacks of chairs.

Equally clear was the illegality of the interior decorations. The firemen could see at once from the intensity of the conflagration that the inside was covered with highly inflammable polystyrene and plastic, against all regulations.

The total absence of internal fire-fighting equipment was another offence for which no explanation could be given. Although French regulations leave the type and exact nature to the discretion of club owners, a list of what is installed goes to the local town hall in all cases and must be approved before building permission is granted. The Cinq-Sept mysteriously got round this rule.

115

Above *Crowds of relatives wait anxiously outside the smouldering ruins for news of their children.*
Right *The funeral ceremony in the gymnasium at St Laurent du Pont. Nineteen bodies remained unidentified.*

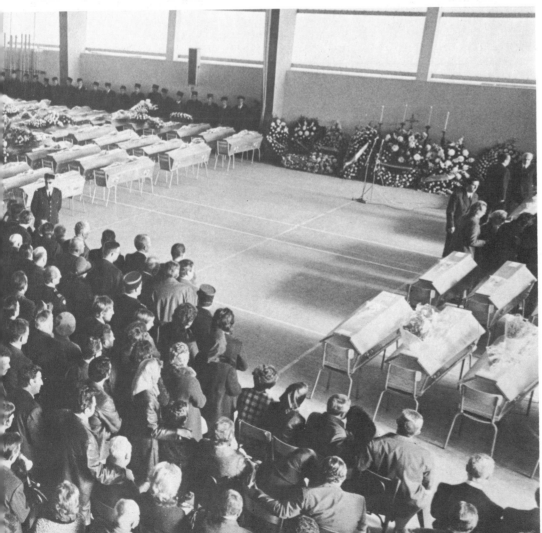

*Above A sad reminder of
the club's original happy
purpose: metal frames from
the band's loudspeaker
equipment survived the
holocaust.*

And, the absence of an on-the-spot telephone was an obvious oversight. Although no regulation compels a club to install one, the very situation of the Cinq-Sept in an isolated spot outside St Laurent du Pont made a telephone a necessity by all rules of common sense.

It hardly needed a detailed or long drawn-out investigation to show that many people were jointly responsible for the Cinq-Sept disaster. Yet so many official bodies were involved—police, safety offices, building departments and so on—that the enquiry soon threatened to bog down in a morass of buck-passing. The Mayor, Pierre Perrin, and the Secretary-General of the Prefecture de l'Isère, Albert Ulrich, were suspended immediately in a mounting wave of public frustration.

Meanwhile, on November 3, a simple funeral ceremony took place in the gymnasium at St Laurent du Pont. One hundred and forty-two coffins were laid out in long rows. All the village shops were shut; hardly any local family was unaffected by the disaster. A small altar was decked with flowers from all over the world, from M. Pompidou, M. Chaban-Delmas and other members of the Government. The room was too small even for just the relatives of the dead. Afterwards, those identified were taken to their home towns and villages to be buried. Nineteen unidentified victims remained at St Laurent du Pont where a special plot had been reserved for them.

On November 6, 1970, Minister of the Interior Raymond Marcellin announced officially that the safety and building regulations had not been observed. The Cinq-Sept had not been inspected by the fire department and had been opened to the public without the official authority of the Mayor. In June 1971 the Mayor and two building contractors were charged with causing injury through negligence. Gilbert Bas, the surviving owner, was charged with manslaughter. In November 1971, all were found guilty but received suspended sentences, Bas for two years, Mayor Perrin for ten months, and three building contractors for 15, 13 and 10 months each.

But the verdicts left many parents dissatisfied, and certainly did nothing to allay fears that such a disaster could easily be repeated. According to the Court, the Cinq-Sept was 'a material illustration of everything forbidden by regulations'. Why did not one responsible authority check up or notify any of the others about the club's total unsuitability to operate? The appropriate authorities never got 'official' notice that the building had been finished, although it opened in March 1970 and advertized in local newspapers and on boardings all over the area. In fact, it was reported that three days before the fire, on October 27, the Commander of Police in Grenoble had been a guest at the Club with various other local worthies. Mayor Perrin was the only public official hauled up because it was easy to pinpoint his failure in the overall pattern of authority. But the real cause of the St Laurent du Pont disaster was sheer bureaucratic inefficiency: too many turning a blind eye to their duties. However tight regulations about building, safety or fire prevention became, the element of incompetence can never be ruled out.

The St Laurent du Pont fire finally claimed 146 victims. Two people were added to the original death list when they died later from severe burns. It was the worst fire in French history, including a blaze in 1921 in the Paris department store Le Printemps which killed 120 people. The worst fire in the world took place in a theatre in Canton, China in 1845, when 1670 people lost their lives in one building.

BRAZIL

São Paulo

February 1, 1974
Office fire in
Sao Paulo

Two hundred and twenty people died in a fire that broke out on the eleventh floor of an office skyscraper in Sao Paulo, Brazil, on February 1, 1974. The city, one of the largest in South America, has a population of 6,000,000, yet it had only 13 fire stations and its equipment proved totally incapable of fighting the blaze or of preventing the shockingly high death toll. (Chicago, a city of almost the same size, has 300 fire stations.) And investigations after the fire revealed that the building had virtually no regulation fire escapes.

The fire probably broke out in an overheated air-conditioning vent. It spread with frightening rapidity because the building's interior was made almost entirely of highly-inflammable materials. The first six floors of the Joelma Building, as it was named, were occupied by a multi-storey car park. Above were the offices of the Crefisul Bank, whose 650 employees and customers were soon cut off by the spreading flames. An eyewitness told how, within minutes, people were running out of the building with their hair in flames. 'Others just stood there petrified and did not move until the flames swallowed them up.' Several people were trampled to death on that first stampede for safety.

Soon, access to the ground through the interior was cut off as the fire created an impenetrable

Below Victims trapped in the blazing Joelma building are pushed by the intense flames to the ledges of the top floors. Two hundred and twenty people died in one of the world's worst urban fires.

barrier. Hundreds of terrified people had no alternative but to retreat upwards to the top floors of the building, but it was a hopeless solution as the flames licked their way higher, sending up clouds of eye-smarting, throat-grabbing smoke.

It must have become clear to the authorities that very few people were going to be rescued, and live television coverage of the feeble rescue attempt was allowed, which aroused those compulsive sensations of fascination and horror which are among the most unattractive of human reactions. 300,000 cars soon jammed the nearby streets as the fire worsened and the victims took desperate measures to escape the flames.

The only hope was to jump. The fire services could not reach people on the higher levels because the ladders were too short. Helicopters, waiting to try to pick people off the roof could not get near for two hours because the flames and smoke were too intense: the paint peeled off the helicopter doors. One after another, people threw themselves out of top-floor windows or off the roof, preferring instant death to slow pain. One man plunged screaming 'Goodbye, goodbye . . .'

Some firemen made heroic efforts to save the trapped by swinging across on ropes from build-

Left A victim jumps from the devouring flames while firemen look on helplessly. The fire fighting equipment available was totally useless to help those trapped above the first few floors of the skyscraper, and there were no other adequate means of escape.
Above right Sao Paulo is one of Brazil's largest cities, with a population of 6 million and a high density of tall buildings, yet it had only 13 fire stations when the Joelma fire occurred.
Right The least attractive aspect of disaster reactions: thousands of spectators crowd the streets and watch the panic-stricken victims drop helplessly from the roof and upper storeys. This morbid interest resulted in more than 300,000 abandoned cars, which blocked the access and exit of the fire equipment and of ambulances carrying the injured.

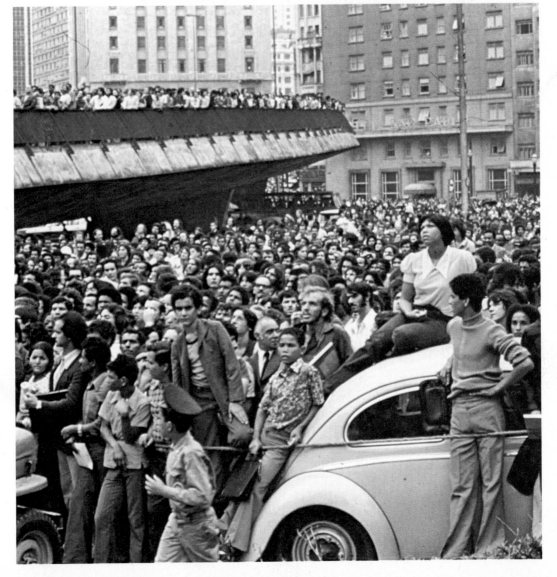

ings close enough to let them reach. One, Sergeant José Rufino, grabbed 18 survivors in this way, swinging on to the window sills and back again. But his bravery almost resulted in his death when he collided with a man falling from the sixteenth floor. The man clinging to Rufino's back was knocked away and fell, but the sergeant managed to retain his grip and get back to safety.

The helicopters could not land till the flames died down but they dropped cartons of milk to the trapped victims on the roof, who were suffering acutely from the acrid smoke fumes rising all around them. Later, about 100 survivors were plucked off by helicopters. Two hundred and fifty people were taken to hospital, including those who ran out or miraculously survived their leaps.

Firemen tried to stop people from jumping by displaying a huge placard with the words, 'Courage, we are with you'. But far too few of the trapped resisted the panic of the situation. A priest, ready to help those he could, was in tears as he said, 'I was not able to get there in time to give last rites to any of them.' Many died instantly. Some stretched out desperately for the ropes thrown down by the helicopters before a landing was possible and died because they could not reach and missed their footing.

The Director of Public Safety, General Servulo Vota Melo, confessed the true nature of Sao Paulo's situation: 'We really lack the necessary equipment to cope with a fire of this magnitude'. The Mayor, Miguel Colasuonno, repeated several times in the confusion of publicity that followed the event, that new building regulations would immediately come into operation. But the city's resources are not even adequate to make a proper analysis of the inflammable materials used in the Joelma Building. Joao Milanez, director of the Police Technical Department, admitted that there are not enough laboratories to administer a preventive scheme for building materials. He suggested that if necessary, the work would be done abroad.

It took the firemen four hours to get the fire under control, and at one stage they considered evacuating nearby buildings in case the Joelma collapsed. Most of the interior from the twelfth floor upwards was burned out, with hunks of charred wood and twisted metal piled on the sodden floors.

There was talk of sabotage in local newspapers at the time. The rumours were given strength when a telephonist at the Crefisul bank said she had received an anonymous call the day before saying that a bomb would explode on Friday morning. But the story was not taken up by the officials conducting the enquiry. It hardly seems necessary to construct an elaborate plot in order to find the guilty parties. Whoever or whatever caused the fire, its casualties are a public indictment of the city's administration. Building regulations, safety precautions and fire-fighting services are hopelessly inadequate. Sao Paulo, in the forefront of Brazil's economic boom, can use no excuse like lack of funds.

Left Only when the fierce heat of the blaze had died down could army helicopters get close enough to lift off a small number of survivors who had managed to make their way to the building's roof.

Ermenonville

Paris

FRANCE

March 3, 1974
The crash of the Turkish DC10

The DC10 crash at Ermenonville near Paris on March 3, 1974, was the worst in the history of civil aviation. The plane, operated by the Turkish national airline Turk Hava Yollari (THY), had arrived in Paris from Istanbul with 117 passengers aboard. There, 217 others joined the flight. Many of them had been booked with British Airways to fly to London, but changed flights because of a strike by groundstaff at Heathrow Airport. The DC10 left Paris on the normal scheduled departure route, climbing up to about 12,000 feet as it headed northeast across France. Suddenly a violent noise indicated decompression and a new sound began in the plane's engines. The plane zoomed forward with increased speed and, 1 minute and 17 seconds after losing internal pressure, plunged to the ground in Ermenonville Forest. It was just five miles from the new Charles de Gaulle airport, where an 11,000-foot runway would have been available. As it fell the plane disintegrated into hundreds of fragments, cutting a swathe 3000 feet long through the trees and scattering bits of luggage and bodies everywhere.

There had been no radio message from the aircraft to say that anything unusual had occurred. The only clue to the cause of the crash came from the French northern regional control centre, where at 12.42 officers had seen two specks on their radar screens; one moving, one stationary. The moving dot could have been the aircraft, the motionless one various items falling from the aircraft, including the rear cargo door and two passengers in their seats, later found a great distance away from the final resting place of the rest of the wrecked plane.

Three hundred and thirty-four passengers and 12 crew members were killed instantly. Rescuers, who took three hours to reach the site because of its inaccessibility, found debris and bits of bodies scattered for miles. No single air crash had caused such high mortality before. The highest death toll previously confirmed was from the crash of a Royal Jordanian Airlines 707 on January 22, 1973, at Kano, Nigeria killing 171 people.

An investigation board to determine the cause of the disaster was established at once. The crash took place on French soil; it was therefore the responsibility of French authorities to look into the facts. A board headed by René Lemair, the inspector general for civil aviation for the Secretariat General, Civil Aviation (SGAC), allowed American and British experts to join, representing the various interests involved. A separate American team from the National Transportation Safety Board came to give their expert help as technical advisors.

The discovery of the cargo hatch cover at the start of the wreckage trail immediately led to speculation that the cause of the crash was decompression due to failure of this door. It had happened before: on June 12, 1972, another DC10, operated by American Airlines, had developed decompression when the cargo door fell off at 11,750 feet and the rear cabin floor buckled in the resulting outrush of air. This in turn jammed the

Number 2 engine cables running under the floor, while the door had smashed into the port tailfin as it ripped away, damaging its mechanism. It was due only to amazing skill that the pilot, Captain Bruce McCormick, turned the plane around and, by using only the ailerons—the levelling control devices on a plane's wingtips—landed at Windsor, Ontario, without further mishap.

Within days of this first suggestion about the cause, some disturbing facts about the Turkish DC10's history emerged. These have helped to turn the crash into one of the worst examples of top level mismanagement and disregard for public safety that has been seen in a multi-national high-finance world such as civil aviation.

DC10s are a new class of aircraft, the wide-bodied jets, and along with the Boeing 747 jumbo and the Lockheed TriStar, carry half the world's long distance passengers. In 1974 a total of 31 airlines were flying 128 DC10s. The THY plane was one of a batch of six originally ordered by the Japanese Mitsui Corporation, who failed to complete the purchase. Instead the six planes were sold to THY and Laker Airways. The planes' manufacturer was the American firm of McDonnell Douglas, formed by merger in 1967. One of the most profitable companies in the business, the firm has a reputation for excellent design and safety in production.

But a central mystery remained unanswered, and the finding of the French enquiry on this point was eagerly awaited. After the Ontario crash, the American National Transportation Safety Board sent various recommendations to the Federal Aviation Administration, the official body governing the operation of aircraft in the USA. The NTSB wanted certain modifications made to the DC10 and hoped the FAA would issue an 'airworthiness directive' which would have legally required McDonnell Douglas and all DC10 operators to comply with the changes required. But no directive was issued. Instead McDonnell Douglas were allowed to send private 'service bulletins' to all companies that had bought the DC10, suggesting various alterations. None were as basic and crucial as those the NTSB had requested. This in itself was a peculiar state of affairs: bulletins are not compulsory, whereas directives are, and the alterations seemed vital for a safely operating DC10. Even stranger was the discovery that the aircraft sold to Turkish Airlines came out of McDonnell Douglas' own factory after the bulletin was issued without the modifications being made to it. McDonnell Douglas President John Brizendine has said, 'This is a circumstance to which we do not yet have an explanation'. Both the THY and a Laker airplane had records stamped by the same persons in the factory, and they had since moved from their jobs.

What were the key modifications required by the National Transportation Safety Board? Most important was improvement of the cargo door. After the Ontario crash, the NTSB looked at it closely and found that the locking mechanism could operate defectively. If the handle was forced, the door gave the appearance of being firmly closed and engaged an electrical safety circuit so that no warning light flashed on the pilot's control panel. But in fact, it was possible for the 'teeth' on the lock to be only half in place. When a plane with an unlocked door climbed to about 12,000 feet, air pressure inside would build up and force the door open. The impact of the escaping air would be enough to buckle the floor of the cargo compartment, damaging vital engine cables running beneath. It could also cause such swift decompression that luggage, seats and passengers might be sucked out through the hole.

From May 1972 to October 1973 McDonnell Douglas and the NTSB had a long correspondence over changes to be made to the door, and the firm periodically issued bulletins requesting operators to make modifications. The NTSB wanted the door altered so it could not be forced. The compartment is used to stow late baggage, and it often happens that a junior airport crewman is responsible for closing it and might do so inexpertly. Also, the NTSB wanted special 'relief vents' built between the cabin and the cargo compartments to lessen the effect of pressure and to prevent the dramatic buckling effect that damages the controls if the plane is de-pressurized.

These were the requests passed to the FAA by the NTSB. The FAA have stated that they believed McDonnell Douglas' own service bulletins were making sufficient changes to cope with the problems without the need for a directive. By August 1972 various bulletins had been issued, ranging from ordering a special window to be placed in the door so that the locking device could be checked to adding notices outside the door giving detailed instructions how to close it. The NTSB seemed reasonably satisfied by these steps, but continued pushing for modifications to the venting system and to the positioning of the essential engine cables under the floor. In March 1973 the FAA informed the NTSB that McDonnell Douglas were still considering these changes but might not find them 'feasible'. In early 1974 the FAA were still awaiting McDonnell Douglas' views on the matter.

For its own part McDonnell Douglas were reluctant to have any of the changes made by FAA directives. There would undoubtedly be bad publicity for its comparatively recent design, and the company believed that the DC10 was as safe as it could be, given existing knowledge in the field of big jets. If the FAA wanted research done into the general area of wide-bodied aircraft, McDonnell Douglas felt it should be government-funded and industry-wide. There was no reason, as far as the management could see, why they alone should carry the task.

Now McDonnell Douglas is facing the biggest lawsuit in the history of civil aviation. A number of passengers' relatives are suing the firm for negligence in its home state of California, where the damages awarded could run to millions of dollars. The DC10 crash has brough to light yet another source of confusion and controversy: unlike sea or rail travel, where passengers are responsible for their own insurance cover and the carriers are not liable in cases of death through negligence, in America airline companies can be held responsible. McDonnell Douglas are not admitting negligence in the matter of design, but have admitted that the cargo door was not modified before it left the factory. However, they are counter-claiming against Turkish Airlines for negligence through its agent, the cargo handler who closed the door.

Unfortunately the position of the bereaved relatives in the lawsuit depends on the convention to which their country belongs. The Warsaw Convention of 1929, updated in 1966 in Montreal, gives claiming parties up to £30,000 damages. Turkish Airlines are not party to the Warsaw agreement, though France and the UK are, and the amount of damages depends on the point of departure, on where a passenger bought his ticket and what conditions were printed on it. A relative might claim as much as £30,000 under the Montreal agreement or as little as £4362 under the original Warsaw convention with various other sums and rules in between.

Three days after the crash the FAA did issue a firm directive to all DC10 operators. The modifications previously requested by McDonnell Douglas are now mandatory for all DC10s in service. The complicated legal battle will hopefully result in a comprehensive international agreement about the legal position of all passengers, operators and plane manufacturers and a tightening of insurance regulations.

Below Three hundred and thirty-four passengers and 12 crew died instantly in the crash. Many relatives came to the scene shortly afterwards to pay their respects to the dead.

Left *The plane's body fragmented when it crashed to the ground. A sudden loss of pressure occurred when a baggage compartment door which had not been properly closed flew open in mid-air.*

Above and below right *The tedious and grueling task of gathering together remnants of personal possessions was necessary so that a complete list of the passengers could be compiled. Hundreds of police and military personnel combed the forest for several days after the crash.*

April 2 and 3, 1974
The 'Ohio' tornadoes

Wednesday and Thursday, April 2 and 3, 1974 saw the worst tornadoes in the American Midwest since 1925. From Decatur, Alabama, to Windsor, Ontario, across the Canadian border, a series of about 100 tornadoes or 'twisters' as they are popularly called struck no less than 11 states. Within eight hours, 324 lives were lost and $400 million in property was destroyed, enough damage for President Nixon to declare five states as disaster areas.

Mortality and damage were probably increased because some of the worst hit areas lie outside the region where tornadoes most commonly occur. In the 'tornado belt' of the Midwest, where twisters are commonplace, the populations are better educated about basic safety precautions and structural design is more likely to allow for

Below Traffic on a highway in Cincinnati speeds on its way in an attempt to drive out of the path of the tornado hovering above. This was one of a series of nearly 100 'twisters' that hit the American Midwest in April 1974.

tornado activity. Xenia Ohio, which suffered the greatest damage, had only experienced seven in the last 24 years, and Brandenburg Kentucky, hit almost as severely, had none in the same time period.

What is a tornado? Usually localized in their effects, 'twisters' cover 200 yards to a mile in area at one time and create a path from five to fifty miles in length, travelling at speeds up to 75mph. The terrifying nature of tornadoes is their unpredictability. They can double back on themselves, take sudden turns left or right or even go round in circles. In the USA they usually affect the Gulf and Midwestern states. The 1974 tornadoes were unusual in travelling so far from south to north, in so short a time, and so far to the east. Tornadoes most frequently occur be-

tween March and July, and statistics put them most frequently between 4.00 and 6.00 pm.

Tornadoes are formed by the peculiar weather effects created when hot air masses from the Gulf of Mexico meet cold polar air masses from the Rocky Mountains that cross into the Midwest. The hot air is trapped beneath a blanket of cold air and cannot rise in its usual way. Sometimes the hot air finds a 'hole' in the blanket and swirls upwards, making currents as it goes. It also cools as it rises, forming clouds and eventually rain.

If this action is rapid then great disturbance soon develops, with dark skies, swirling rain and wind, hailstones and thunderstorms. Static electricity is produced by the great mass of energy.

At this stage people on the ground can recognize the warning signs of a tornado—a looming black cloud hangs high in the sky, sudden gusts of wind shake trees and walls and the air temperature increases ominously, becoming clammy and close. The minute the 'vortex' of the tornado appears, destruction is near. This whiplash tail or funnel-shaped spiral of whirling air is the centre of the tornado's energy. As soon as it touches the ground, the partial vacuum at the heart of the vortex and the fierce whirling winds literally suck up and blast apart anything in their path. An American expert describes the effect of these terrible forces: 'bark has been peeled off trees, harnesses have been stripped off horses, and clothing has been stripped off people leaving them completely naked. Dead sheep have been found shorn of their wool, feathers have been plucked off chickens . . .'

In Xenia, Ohio, the worst-hit town in the 1974 disaster, whole buildings were ripped apart and left like piles of matchsticks. As a tornado passes over a building, the near-vacuum or low pressure area in its funnel exerts a great tug on the rooms below, where the air is of a higher pressure. This air is forced upwards and outwards, blowing the house apart with all the force of a dynamite explosion. Half of Xenia was levelled in this way. Metal street signs were bent back on their poles like flags frozen in a double fold. A van stood in a deserted street—undamaged but for every window blown out clean. A truck was lifted out of a driveway, forced into a tree which it uprooted, and put down upside down on top of it. A train passing through Xenia at that fatal moment was loaded with a consignment of brand new Mustang cars. Every one was dented and full of broken glass. Days later, bundles of bank notes from the smashed bank were found 200 miles away at Cayahoga Falls.

One Xenia family found a vivid example of the tornado's capriciousness in the laundry room of their house, destroyed except for one wall. Splintered wood had been driven through the metal clothes pole; the clothes dryer had been jammed with flying dishes. But an open box of soap powder stood undisturbed on top of the washing machine, exactly as it had been left.

William Hitchcock, a Xenia jeweller, could

Below Splinters of wood litter the ground for miles around destroyed homesteads in Hanover, Indiana, which suffered more damage from the tornadoes than had been felt there in 50 years.

point to the exact time the tornado hit: the hands of the clock in his street sign, bent and twisted, stood still at 4.40pm. 'It sounded like a fast passenger train. It was really just filling the air with stuff, really violent.'

Another Xenia citizen saw the dark cloud in the distance:

'Then all of a sudden it must have touched down. There was a whole mess of confetti going up from the ground. A warm rain started and I knew it was time to go.

'I went into the house and just then I felt the wind kick. We—there were seven of us—got down on the floor of the kitchen . . . then all the windows went all at once, you could hear them breaking all over the house. Then all I could hear was the wind. Mud and glass were flying around and hitting everybody. The rushing wind went on and on. All you could hear was the wind'.

When this man crawled out of his house all the roofs were gone and almost no second storeys were left on any of the houses around.

When the tornado had passed by, people emerged and began picking at the wrecks of their homes, as if gathering firewood, dazed and totally silent. Some just sat. One elderly lady wrapped in a blanket sat in a rocking chair. The roof had blown off her house, but she would not move nor speak for several hours.

The path of destruction across Xenia, nearly one mile wide and three miles long, had been scythed through in five minutes. Out of the 25,000 population, 30 people were dead and thousands homeless. Gas, electricity and telephone services were cut off: dangerous live wires hung from twisted pylons and poles.

The injured, numbering at least 80 were taken to Miami Valley Hospital in Dayton ten miles away; and Ohio's National Guard soon moved in with bulldozers, emergency rations and medical supplies to restore order as soon as possible. Three-quarters of the town's electricity supply was restored by the next day. With contemptuous disregard for the homeless, nature sent a snowstorm to the town on April 5, immediately after the tornado had passed.

The picture of destruction in Xenia was repeated across all the eleven states affected. Alabama, Kentucky, Ohio, Indiana and Tennessee were all declared disaster areas, making massive federal aid available for immediate rescue and rehabilitation programmes, and low-interest loan systems were devised to help businesses.

Kentucky was almost as badly afflicted as Ohio. Seventy-one people died in the state, 29 of them in the small Ohio River town of Brandenburg, 32 miles west of Louisville. Between six and seven thousand homes in the vicinity were made uninhabitable or completely destroyed. Brandenburg itself almost totally disappeared. In Louis-

Below Within eight hours, 324 lives had been lost and $400 million in property had been reduced to rubble. President Nixon declared five states official disaster areas.

ville, the roof was ripped off a school building, and the engine lifted out of a car parked outside by rotational winds estimated at speeds of 200 mph. Much greater tragedy would have ensued if the town's several thousand schoolchildren had not gone home just before the tornado came. Most of the dead were children playing outside.

In Kentucky, insurance claims were estimated at $81.5 million, and Governor Wendell Ford described it 'probably the most tragic day in Kentucky history'.

Indiana lost 22 lives, and many of its smaller population centres were wiped out, like Depaun, home of 500 people. Borden, Hamburg and Martinsburg were 60 percent destroyed. In Fountainstown, eight houses and a fire station were obliterated and a metal frame manufacturing factory's warehouse was lifted off the ground and carried a mile away.

A similar incident caused the death of a man in Virginia when the wind picked up his mobile home, hurled it 100 yards and deposited it upside-down in a wrecked heap. His wife was thrown clear, but suffered some injuries in her fall.

The state of Indiana was severely affected in the south around Hanover, and at Rochester and Monticello in the north-central part. Damage to this area was estimated at $100 million. In Monticello, an elderly lady estimated that the tornado took less than one minute to cross the town.

Above left The whiplash tail of the tornado is the centre of the storm's energy. As soon as it touches ground, the partial vacuum at the heart of the vortex and the fierce winds suck up and destroy everything in its path.
Below Victims of disasters are often stunned and incapable of action while they mentally digest the full impact and reality of what has happened to them.

Left *This mother in Xenia, Ohio was reunited with her three children 17 hours after the tornadoes struck. Many victims of disaster will not accept that relatives or close friends are safe until they can actually hold them and get physical reassurance.*
Below *Reputedly the first-ever photograph of a tornado, taken about 1880.*

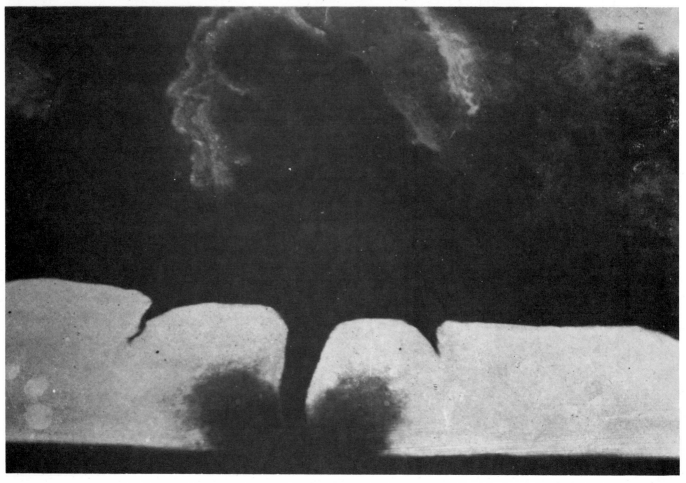

'When it had gone I lost everything. My furniture looks like a pile of firewood', she ended.

The National Guard in Indiana had to divert 1000 men to the task of keeping out sightseers, who hampered the relief work. Every truck in the state left in working order was commandeered to help distribute needed supplies.

In Alabama, there was widespread destruction of main lines of communication. The town of Jasper lost most of its main street, its city hall was demolished and its stone courthouse left in a dangerously shattered state. A radio announcer at the local station told his audience: 'We can't talk to the police department—it just blew away.'

There seems very little that could have been done to prevent this widespread destruction. Since the early 1950s, tornadoes have killed an average of 123 people a year. The National Oceanic and Atmospheric Administration said that it had given as much warning as it could, but the unpredictable nature of tornadoes means that they cannot be controlled or prevented.

Ohio was one of the states affected by the last severe tornado strike, on Palm Sunday, April 11, 1965. Thirty-seven separate 'twisters' struck the Midwest, killing 271 people and injuring 5000 more. In 1931 a tornado in Minnesota carried an 83-ton railway carriage and its 117 passengers 80 feet through the air and dropped them in a ditch. Worst of all was the March 18, 1925, disaster, when one single giant tornado ripped through Mississippi, Illinois and Indiana, killing 689 people and injuring hundreds more.

There is very little anyone can do to protect a building that falls right in a tornado's path. The safest place is in a basement or 'storm cellar' specially constructed for tornado shelter. If you are caught in the open, your best chance for survival is to lie down in a ditch or the deepest hollow available. The driver of a car can sometimes steer out of the path of a tornado, but if the vehicle is actually caught, it will be reduced to scrap metal.

If there is no time to get to shelter, the safest place in a building is away from windows to avoid injury from flying glass, and underneath a strong piece of furniture such as a bureau or table which can provide some protection from missiles of debris. Doors and windows on the side of the house facing away from the tornado's path can be left open to try to equalize the pressure, thereby reducing damage to the building. It is never advisable to take shelter in big open-area buildings with weak roof structures, like school gymnasiums and indoor swimming pools.

The only preventive measure that gives any real hope of lessening the destruction caused by tornadoes is to improve the early warning system, so that people are given time to get to shelter and can be kept informed about the path that a tornado is likely to take. Just before the 1974 disaster, the National Oceanic and Atmospheric Administration had asked Congress for an extra $16 million to do just that.

Below The funnel-shaped cloud of another tornado rips its way across Texas. These killer winds, which can reach a speed of 400 mph, are particularly prevalent in the Midsouth and Midwest, especially in the months between March and July.

June 1, 1974
Explosion at Flixborough

ENGLAND

Hull

Flixborough

Twenty-nine people died and more than 100 were injured when the UK's worst industrial explosion devastated the Nypro plant at Flixborough, near Scunthorpe, on June 1, 1974. One hundred homes in the village were destroyed or badly damaged, and the force of the blast was so great that it could be heard 30 miles away. The Nypro plant was gutted by a fire that broke out immediately following the explosion and raged uncontrollably all day. It was still burning 24 hours later. Only eight badly charred bodies of the 29 dead could be recovered; 27 were Nypro employees, another a sub-contractor and the last an outside driver who happened to be at the factory when it blew up. The disaster occurred late on a Saturday afternoon when a reduced staff of 70 were on duty. Otherwise the death toll could have been enormous, for the firm employed a total of 550 people.

The explosion caused widespread surprise since chemical factories built on this massive scale were supposed to be so well protected in building design and safety procedure that accidents of this sort could not happen. Immediate clues to the cause came from the reports of a few eye witnesses.

Tom McCale, a chemist technician working in one of the labs saw a flash and then glimpsed flames licking along a trail of leaking gas. He shouted to his seven colleagues to get out, and they all ran out of the lab in one direction while he turned another way, right into the force of the explosion. He suffered serious concussion and was taken to hospital.

Another worker who escaped from the part of the plant where the explosion originated, Area One, was Lawrence Harry: 'I heard a bang, quickly followed by a large explosion. Everything went black as hell. I was picked up and thrown 30 yards. We were wandering about in a daze. One of our friends was missing so we went back inside to get him.'

From outside the plant, descriptions from onlookers give some impression of just how devastating the blast was. One man in Scunthorpe, six miles away, told how 'it parted the clouds and went up like a mushroom as though an atom bomb had exploded'. In the village of Flixborough roofs were torn off houses, windows blown out and walls cracked. People in the street were badly injured by flying glass imbedded in their flesh, so violent was the impact. Some were picked up and hurled against walls or cars. A local housewife expressed the shock of most of her friends: 'It went up like an H-bomb in mushrooms with two circles. I never expected anything like this. I never realized there was such a danger.'

Her comment sums up public reaction to Flixborough. The villagers around the Nypro plant had never been told about the process or its inherent risks.

Nypro Limited was owned jointly by the British National Coal Board and the Dutch State Mining Company—Holland's equivalent to the

Previous page Acrid fumes and uncontrollable flames pour out of the Flixborough Nypro plant. An explosion in which 29 people died was caused by a leaky gas pipe.
Left The blast blew out windows and injured several people in nearby villages. The local inhabitants had little idea of the potential danger on their doorstep.

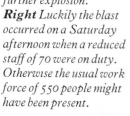

Above left A road sign on the outskirts of the village stands bent by the blast, which could be heard 30 miles away. Most of the homes in Flixborough suffered some damage.

Below left Fire-fighting efforts were hampered by the deadly fumes that poured out of the chemical containers. It took firemen more than 24 hours to get the fire under control.

Above A scene of devastation at Flixborough. Ironically, no one from the village worked at the chemical plant. 3000 people were evacuated for fear of a further explosion.

Right Luckily the blast occurred on a Saturday afternoon when a reduced staff of 70 were on duty. Otherwise the usual work force of 550 people might have been present.

NCB. The Flixborough plant was the single manufacturing centre in the UK for caprolactam, a key ingredient in the manufacture of nylon. The history of the plant exemplifies modern industrial development through competition. The British firm of Courtaulds had been excluded from the expanding field of nylon manufacture because its rival ICI and the American giant Du Pont had a firm grip on the only known process for making nylon fibre, patented 'Nylon 66'.

Then in the early 1960s, the Dutch State Mining Company found a new way to make almost the same product, which they called 'Nylon 6'. At first they went into partnership with Fisons, an English fertilizer company, who were interested in a by-product of the new process. But as DSM improved its methods, this by-product was reduced in quantity, and Fisons dropped out. DSM then turned to a similar organization as its new partner and the NCB stepped in.

At that time the joint venture was supplying Courtaulds with 20,000 tons of caprolactam, the chemical used to make nylon. The National Coal Board became 45 per cent owners in May 1969. Gradually the process was simplified and speeded up until at the time of the accident the plant produced 70,000 tons a year, an annual output worth £18m. However, greater hazards crept into the process. The plants operated by DSM under licence in North and South America used a slightly longer system, but from 1973 the Flixborough plant involved a short cut, using benzene rather than cyclohexane to start the process. It is cheaper, but it is also highly toxic, inflammable and explosive.

The crucial moment in the manufacture of caprolactam comes after the benzene has been used to produce cyclohexane. This chemical is then mixed with ammonia in an oxidizing plant. The cyclohexane is under great pressure at this stage, and the supply of oxygen must be very precisely controlled. What comes out is cyclohexanone oxide, which is treated with concentrated sulphuric acid or phosphoric acid at the isomerizing plant. This produces caprolactam, which in turn produces 'Nylon 6'.

From all accounts it looked as if the explosion had resulted from a leak in a gas pipe which ignited immediately. Cyclohexane is like petrol in the safety problems it presents; 1000 tons were stored at Flixborough at the time. Regular precautions included searching employees for lighters, cigarettes and matches, and issuing special footwear for use in certain areas of the plant. But, as one expert pointed out, even the static electricity created by wearing a nylon shirt on a warm day could provide the spark to cause a fire if there was an undetected leak.

Although the explosion caused more death and damage than any previous in peacetime, it did not come totally unheralded. In September 1973 Brian Harvey, the chief inspector of factories, had published the annual report of the Inspectorate and gave the following clear warning in his introduction: 'We may well see a continuing fall in the fatal accident rate, while at the same time we are faced increasingly with the risk of failures which could result in multiple deaths and injuries of near-disaster proportions.' As a result of Mr Harvey's recommendations, a new bill 'Health and Safety at Work' was on its way to becoming an act of Parliament at the time of the Flixborough explosion.

Its proposals seem so commonsensical that it is cause for wonder that nothing of the sort had become law before. The prime task of the bill was to reform the jumble of long-standing rules and regulations that cover industrial hazards, many of which date back to the middle of the nineteenth century. At least six different Government authorities watchdog factory building and operation. Industrial plants, mines, agricultural sites, nuclear installations and explosives manufacturing are all separately governed. The bill sought to put all these together in one uniform organization. It also provided that employers should inform their work force and people living in the immediate vicinity about the nature of possible hazards and the degree of risk involved. Unions would be empowered to place representatives on a factory safety committee, to put forward the workers' opinions and express any fears.

Something at least was being done, but another area of doubt and confusion was opened up by the Flixborough disaster. The plant was the sole UK supplier of caprolactam. It provided the basic raw material for an industry employing 30,000 people, making goods as varied as nylon stockings, carpet backing, seat belts and tyres. All these jobs were threatened by the closure of the plant. As there was a world shortage of caprolactam supplies anyway, there was little chance of the manufacturers affected being able to switch their orders to other plants. In one day, June 3, Courtaulds lost £20 million off its stock market value, because it was one of Nypro's biggest customers.

Industrial experts argue that giant-scale operations like Flixborough are a good thing. They are cheaper to operate than numerous small factories dotted about, because they cut down transport and manufacturing costs. Raw ingredients can be bought more cheaply in bulk. They provide a job centre for the areas where they are located. But these arguments look only at the economic and business factors, not at social or environmental ones. Flixborough changed that. The validity of building giant plants that can wreak havoc if they explode or allow harmful chemicals to escape is being questioned. Even in pure economic terms, the disastrous consequence of losing a complete supply of a raw material at once, never before taken as a likelihood, is causing serious re-thinking.

One important fact about the Nypro plant is easily overlooked. In Flixborough, population 300, no house was without damage, yet no one from the village worked at the plant. It has always been a quiet, rural community. After

Aberfan, parents protested the decision to leave remaining coal tips where they were; at Flixborough, a local committee was set up to prevent another monster being built in place of the twisted metal ruin. The plant gave off small chemical explosions for a week after June 1. The Flixborough disaster brings into sharp focus the problem of placing a potential hazard near a community which reaps no direct benefits from its presence.

After the initial assessment that a broken pipe allowed a gas leak that caused the explosion, a four-man enquiry headed by Roger Parker QC was set up to look into the overall problem of safety in large-scale plants and to make recommendations. It will consider whether it is better to have gas-filled pipes passing through the open air so that leaks can dissipate harmlessly into the atmosphere, or whether, because of the risk of ignition and explosion, such pipes should be built inside thick walls, to contain any blast. Little research has been done, and one possible result of the enquiry will be to set up a properly-funded experiment.

Industry and technology move forward quickly, sometimes without full realization of possible hazards to society. Plants and factories cannot be built in deserts. When does an industrial development become dangerous? After Flixborough, new criticisms will inevitably be made of oil refineries, chemical plants, even airports and big garages as potentially dangerous. As Inspector of Factories Brian Harvey commented, 'We are running instead of walking. We have to feel our way with these new technologies.'

__Above right__ The Flixborough explosion brought into question the wisdom of large-scale factories. This disaster knocked out the only source in the UK of caprolactam, a substance essential to the manufacture of all kinds of nylon goods.
__Right__ Only eight of the 29 bodies could be recovered from the wrecked plant, so intense was the force of the explosion and the heat of the fire that followed.

CARIBBEAN SEA

HONDURAS

CENTRAL AMERICA

PACIFIC OCEAN

November 18, 1974
Hurricane
Fifi

A giant hurricane swept through Honduras in Central America on the night of Wednesday, November 18, 1974, causing 8000 deaths and destroying the homes of another 10,000 people. The disaster, the greatest of its kind ever to afflict one country, could not have happened in a more unfortunate place. Honduras was virtually a disaster area before Hurricane Fifi arrived. It is the poorest country in the Americas, with a rapidly growing population. The average worker earns no more than about £80 a year.

There had been signs of hurricane build-up off the coast of Honduras two weeks before, but no harm came to the land area that time. When the national radio broadcast heavy rain and high winds warnings in the evening before Fifi arrived, some people did not give the message its real significance. Then, in the dead of night, the hurricane tore up the east coast of Honduras, with winds of up to 140mph smashing the poorly-built houses of farm labourers and torrents of rain dropping 24 inches of water in 36 hours.

The worst hit area was around the town of Choloma where nearly 3000 people died. By Friday morning the dense rainstorms had created an avalanche of flood water. Trees, mud and boulders tore down the Choloma River and destroyed nearly all houses on its banks. Over half the citizens of Choloma died. One survivor, an old man of 76, lost all his family; when he searched the ruins of his home, he found two strange bodies washed into it in a bank of mud. 'I don't know who they were,' he said. 'They were just poor innocents who were swept down the mountain and ended up here.'

More people were killed by the floods and other hazards that followed Hurricane Fifi than by the force of the storm-wind itself. In the area around San Pedro Sula, the second city of Honduras in the northeast of the country, 400,000 people were left homeless and prey to exposure, starvation and disease. So great was the threat of an epidemic of typhoid (endemic in Honduras anyway) that the government ordered the immediate mass burning of bodies to prevent infection. In Choloma about 2700 dead were incinerated. The town was an appalling sight, with bodies lying about in the mud rapidly putrefying in the intense heat that followed the rains and winds of the hurricane. There were other natural hazards too, like snakes and spiders, for fer-de-lances and tarantulas wriggled out of their natural homes in the undergrowth in banana groves, disturbed by the flood waters.

Bananas bring in half of Honduras' foreign exchange, and the giant plantations, mostly owned by American companies, employ 30,000 people. A whole year's crop was destroyed by Fifi, an economic disaster matching the human one in magnitude and severity. Huston Lacombe, manager of the United Fruit Company's Honduran subsidiary, described his company's losses: 'We have 28,000 acres of bananas. Twenty thousand are under water, and five thousand were flattened by winds. The waves lifted the railroad track from its bed on the plantations around La Lima [on the coast] and the company's wharves at Puerto Cortés were badly damaged'.

In the Aguan valley plantations, mostly owned by the Standard Fruit Company, another American concern, were totally destroyed. Floodwater spread seven miles from the river bed itself. The total loss to banana growers in Honduras was estimated to be as high as $150m.

These two companies have stated their intention to rebuild their plantations, but the disaster brought fears that they might pull out altogether. Honduras is desperately poor and its President, General Oswaldo Lopez, had been making firm demands on the largely foreign-owned companies in order to raise extra taxes. Now these organizations face heavy costs for re-establishing their industry and for re-opening the country's only railway, which they own privately. It carries the fruit from the farms to the coast for shipment abroad. Since 13 per cent of the world's bananas come from Honduras, it is possible that the big fruit companies will begin business again on their own terms, not on those of the government, in spite of the country's dependence on this agricultural industry.

What about the surviving victims of Hurricane Fifi? Their fate was to suffer even greater hardship after the disaster. Many were stranded for days, clinging to rooftops, sitting in trees high above the flood, waiting for rescue. Help was long in coming because all bridges, roadways and electricity supplies were wiped out. After a couple of days, American helicopters arrived from bases in the Panama Canal Zone, and in one rescue effort in the countryside around San Pedro Sula, 34 refugees scrambled into a helicopter with normal maximum capacity of 15.

Far left The scene of destruction in Choloma, Honduras, in the wake of Hurricane Fifi. Some 8000 people lost their lives in the worst hurricane ever recorded in the western hemisphere.
Left A satellite weather track of Fifi shows the enormous size of the storm gathering over Honduras.

Gradually food and medical supplies began to arrive in the stricken areas. Two towns were appointed relief centres: Tocoa, 125 miles north-east of the capital, Tegucigalpa, and San Pedro Sula, in the middle of the area worst affected. Rations came from the USA, Great Britain, Mexico, Cuba, and the Central American states nearby. But the threat of starvation was becoming a reality for many. American Ambassador Philip Sanchez commented: 'You ask how people can starve in just three or four days, but these people were hungry even before the disaster.'

The hurricane not only destroyed rich banana groves but also the meagre little strips of farm-land where the fathers of large families in constant want of food eked out subsistence crops. A Honduran relief official, Lt Col. Eduardo Andino, said, 'People are starving, their supplies were washed away and there are no stores near their villages. They have no way to get food except from us.'

Heated accusations began to fly about in the first weeks after the disaster. It was suggested that the Honduran officials had exaggerated the number of lives lost in Hurricane Fifi in order to get more money from foreign aid sources for the languishing economy. The plight of Hondurans alive or dead is so sorry that no amount of over-estimating could produce unfair or unnecessary sums of money.

Yet worse stories emerged about the conduct of the relief programme. The Honduran army

was in charge of the operation, and at times came into conflict with the international organizations trying to run emergency canteens and field hospitals on the spot. Soldiers and Red Cross workers battled over supplies arriving at the airport in San Pedro Sula, as frequently happens in developing countries where corruption and crude political tactics combine to use food and essential medicines as bribes or valuable stockpiled capital. (The same problem arose with the north Andes earthquake, Peru 1970, and the 1972 'quake at Managua, Nicaragua.)

At a local level, efforts to organize relief were muddled and varying in success. In some of the refugee camps that sprang up in a matter of days, central food distribution and canteens proved futile because families persisted in their usual habit of cooking for themselves. Most useful equipment was lost in the mud. The Honduran government had neither the resources nor the expertize to organize a rehabilitation programme on the required scale. There were no bulldozers, cranes or flying doctor outfits, and no emergency stores of food or medical supplies.

Cuba provided one of the most immediate and effective remedies: a field hospital team of about 40 doctors, nurses and orderlies, who set up headquarters in a cattle market. A small stadium there was used to provide beds on stone seats. The main work of the team was to provide immediate injection services to prevent epidemics, simple first aid and food for the injured.

Above left The Tela railroad, privately owned by American banana-growing companies, was washed out by the floods that accompanied the storm. Most of the banana plantations, which grow the major part of the export produce for the whole of Honduras, are situated near San Pedro Sula, the worst-hit town in the country.
Below left At La Ceiba, Honduras, a house carried downstream came to rest precariously astride a damaged bridge.
Above In Choloma 2700 dead bodies had to be incinerated to lower the risk of disease and infection spreading in the sweltering heat that followed the hurricane.

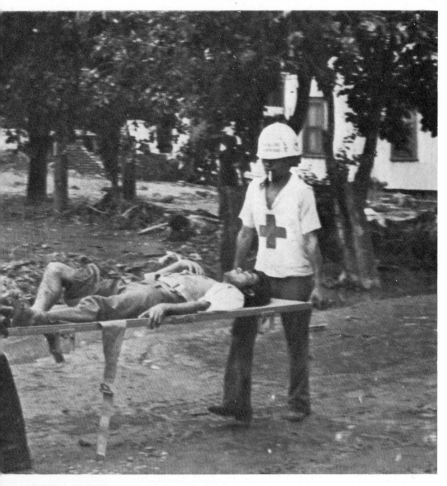

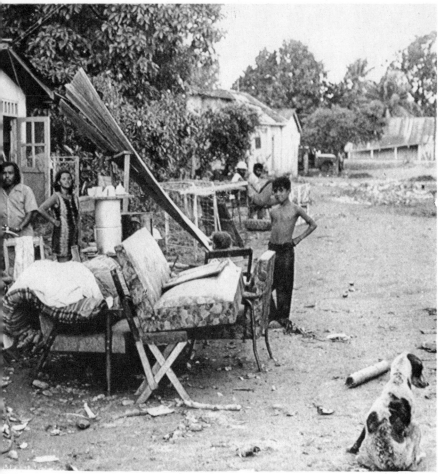

Great Britain sent in troops from nearby Belize and gave army supplies of blankets, camp beds, ten-day rations kits and medicines. £20,000 was sent from the British government, and efforts were co-ordinated through the new Whitehall Disaster Unit under the Ministry for Overseas Development, the first time that the new organization had been put into full operation.

The USA sent helicopters and planes that flew supplies to isolated outlying areas. Peace Corps workers soon had camps and kitchens set up in a more orderly fashion. An international disaster fund was opened to provide money on a long term basis for the work of rehabilitation.

It has been estimated that it will take Honduras at least two years, with foreign aid, to recover. But that would allow only for a return to the position existing before Hurricane Fifi struck. To better the state of the tiny nation will take far longer. For example, the lack of sufficient numbers of relief workers was brought about in part by the fact that the Honduran government would not relieve army garrisons on guard duty along the border with El Salvador. Honduras had a short but disastrous war with this rich neighbouring country in 1969. Afterward she withdrew in protest from the Central American 'common market' and damaged her own chances of economic and social progress, an action which has had disastrous effects.

Perhaps the saddest aspect of the disaster is that the peasants of Honduras probably do not see that some of the blame should lie with political factors, not natural forces. Maria Hernandez, a 54-year-old survivor from Choloma, said in a filmed interview just after the hurricane that she thought the disaster had come as a judgement from God. People were not working hard enough and did not have the right attitude. Her own daughter had been swept away by the floodwater; her last words had been 'God forgive me'.

A belief in divine retribution is common and deepfelt at the time of a catastrophe. After a few days or weeks more realistic and critical reactions set in. Hopefully, General Oswaldo Lopez, who has ruled Honduras since 1963, will find a way out of the country's present ruin before political unrest creates more problems.

Above left In San Pedro Sula, some inhabitants piled their meagre possessions on the roof of their abandoned houses.
Below left A distraught father carries his half-drowned child to safety in San Pedro Sula.
Above right International Red Cross workers were among the first to arrive to help the stranded, sick, homeless and hungry.
Below right An estimated 50,000 people were left without shelter after Hurricane Fifi.
Most Hondurans live on the brink of starvation under normal circumstances, with little physical stamina and no reserves of food or money to help them through such a crisis.

Human reaction to disaster

Disasters present unique conditions to the human beings who are caught up in them and as a result produce emotions and responses which are unlike those experienced at any other time in life. Even wartime creates an atmosphere different from disaster because the event is continuous over days, months or years and is shared by entire populations. Possibly the most distinctive feature of a disaster is that it suddenly hits a particular section of society and isolates them from everyday life. This feeling of being different, singled out by fate, makes people behave in strange ways.

Several separate time spans occur in the disaster cycle, each presenting its own particular problems. The first is that time when something *could* happen, but the prospect is so remote that no steps are taken to prevent it. During this pre-disaster phase, obvious signs of danger are ignored. The period can last for years without anything getting worse, and that in itself encourages the attitude of 'it can't happen to me'. (In her famous study of disaster, American psychologist Martha Wolfenstein describes this as 'a sense of immunity'.) Examining the events described in this book, we see time and again evidence of impending destruction completely overlooked: by the citizens of St Pierre when Mount Pelèe began to rumble; by the engineers at the Vaiont Dam when Mount Toc showed signs of stress; by the Coal Board authorities in South Wales when the Aberfan tip was known to be unstable. Sometimes, denying the existence of danger is a natural way of avoiding anxiety: there may be little precaution that could be taken. Doing nothing at all might be a throwback to a childish dislike of authority, of being told what to do. Many people resist public advice as a matter of 'principle', especially in the case of such natural hazards as tornado or hurricane warnings. When Hurricane Camille hit the Gulf States, many people refused to go to the established Red Cross shelters and threw 'hurricane parties' instead. Some were found dead the following day.

When the disaster approaches and warnings are actually issued, as in the case of tornadoes, floods or sometimes fires, many people enter a second phase: frantic activity. In proportion to how little they did before, they now compensate by trying to do so much that their efforts are not only ineffective, but can lead to chaos. Some people run away because they cannot cope with the impending event. In this phase (as in all others), panic can be alleviated if people are given accurate and non-sensational news about what could happen, so that they have an idea of their options. If information is withheld until the catastrophe occurs as in the 1966 flooding of Florence, adverse reaction is more severe because people have not had a chance to prepare themselves for it. On a more everyday level, the nurse's reassuring words to a surgical patient, 'it'll be all right', instead of a simple explanation of what will happen, can produce fantasies and fears out of scale with the event. This tendency is magnified if an impending disaster is deliberately played down.

The third and central moment of the cycle is the occurrence of the calamity itself. In many cases, such as the Halifax harbour explosion and the fires in Boston and Sao Paulo, it happens without preparation or warning signals. Immediately after the moment of impact, survivors tend to feel that they alone have been affected. Many believe, quite irrationally, that they are being 'punished' by God or by fate. There is a terrible sense of being alone and totally isolated from the rest of the world. If no precautionary steps have been taken, the idea of punishment is clearly felt. The sense of abandonment makes the victim worry desperately about his relatives and friends. In the San Francisco and Tokyo earthquakes, people ran in all directions looking for family and neighbours. Helpers arriving in a disaster area immediately after the event often find that victims will not believe the reassuring words that a child or friend is safe and well. They must see the person, touch him, hug him, before they will believe that everything is all right. In general, the immediate need of the disaster victim is for human comfort—to remind him that he has not been singled out for chastisement.

Sometimes people are so knocked off balance by the gravity of the event that a severe depression sets in. They are dazed and silent and cannot be moved, like the old lady caught in the Ohio tornado who would not budge from her seat amid the ruins of her house for a whole day. Psychologists believe that the event is so enormous to these individuals that it cannot be taken in all at once. So much has happened that no more can be absorbed. And, a disaster undermines man's belief in himself, in his permanence and security. The shock to his sense of well-being leaves him lost and helpless. Such individuals are best helped by gentle communication, by warmth and a hot drink. Eventually a simple task helps bring back a feeling of usefulness and belonging.

After this sense of abandonment and being punished comes an intense gratitude for the help that the victims receive. Unlike accident victims, who tend to complain loudly and are often distraught, disaster victims are quiet, obedient and desperately thankful for attention. Martha Wolfenstein's view is that this again stems from the idea of punishment from on high: now the victim, like a naughty child, is trying to be 'good'. In contrast, some people throw themselves into another stage of frenetic activity, as if trying to make up for their earlier failure to take precautionary steps.

Certainly activity is not useless; disasters produce individual acts of incredible bravery, like the passer-by who saved several women from the Cocoanut Grove night club and the fireman who swung through the air to catch survivors off window sills in the Sao Paulo office fire. Rescue can come from a person of responsibility or from one avoiding thoughts about his own pain. When Captain Max Pruss of the Hindenburg ran back into the flaming wreckage of the airship to search for survivors, there can be no doubt that his thoughts were to his duty. His back badly burned, he had to be 'captured' by three other men and forced to go to hospital. Also, the activity helps to delay the full horror of the event. Many people work till they drop, as in Aberfan, preferring oblivion to letting in the pain.

Some, like Señor Caruso who could never be provoked to recall the San Francisco earthquake, prefer to ignore the entire incident. Generally speaking, avoiding the issue can lead to more severe mental stress. People who will not talk about their experiences may find they go over the event in their dreams for years afterwards. A young man who lost his wife in the Cocoanut Grove fire was at first very cheerful and extremely active. But he later became agitated and blamed himself for her death. He felt he ought to have saved her, and his refusal to come to terms with the event eventually led to his suicide.

Some survivors are over-active and rush about chattering endlessly, often cracking jokes that seem in poor taste to those who come into the area after the event. After the dreadful feeling of isolation and abandonment, a sense of relief and even elation floods in when a person realizes he is not alone. Repeating details of the event to anyone who will listen is a way of getting used to the idea that a disaster has actually happened. If there has been little preparation or anticipation

A classic example of a disaster reaction: as long as a person has his nearest and dearest around him for assurance, he somehow seems to find the nerve and the strength to cope with the most extreme hardships. At the same time most people are unable to take in the full reality of what has occurred and carry on as if nothing has happened. Here, survivors of the San Francisco earthquake enjoy a domestic meal, seemingly oblivious to the wreckage all around them.

beforehand, this process goes on much longer. After the chemical plant explosion at Flixborough, endless tales of what happened were exchanged for weeks later, because local residents had not known about the possibility of danger there.

One dangerous aspect of the 'overactive' response to a disaster is that people who behave in this way can be very argumentative and often are the first to suggest a scapegoat. Where there is tension and distress, irrational suggestions can trigger a chain reaction and lead to panic or mass hysteria. In the aftermath of the Tokyo earthquake, someone raised the absurd notion that the Korean community were responsible for the fires that broke out all over the city, and terrible acts of reprisal were carried out against innocent people.

The total breakdown of ordinary life at the moment of a catastrophe sometimes produces a feeling of lawlessness. The world has gone to pieces; authority is powerless against some greater force of natural evil. Looting, arson, murder or assault are common crimes in post-disaster circumstances, such as after Hurricane Camille.

The final phase of a disaster takes the form of delayed responses. After a period of intense communal activity, involving heroism, self-denial, comradeship and unselfishness, a reversal occurs. This usually coincides with the arrival of outside relief agencies, who are met on occasion with hostility and complaints about unfair distribution of supplies and lack of understanding. The temporary elation and co-operation sets up high expectations for the future of the world as a better place; disappointment is bound to set in. After a period of thinking exclusively about others worse off than himself, the disaster victim begins to realize what he has lost. Wrangles develop about relief funds and compensation payments. Angry calls for a blame centre rise up. Often, like children, people choose to accuse authorities who did not provide proper protection for them. Blaming the force of nature would be terrifying and makes the world seem a very unsafe place. Better to blame someone human and punishable than an uncontrollable agent.

People often return to live on the site of a disaster. Perhaps they feel they are demonstrating defiance or a control of natural forces. They master the situation and their own innermost fears by rebuilding their lives where once chaos reigned. Others feel it is their recompense to those who died. 'You got it last time, but I came back, and who knows, maybe I will be the next.' Of course, in the case of natural phenomenon like earthquakes, people's attachment to their home and birthplace may simply outweigh all possible danger. This appears to be one of the strongest ties that binds people to localities.

One of the greatest difficulties faced by relief agencies and disaster prevention units is the sense of immunity mentioned earlier. 'It's happened here once; we won't get it again,' people think. The reverse is often the case, but some primitive sense of the law of averages or natural justice often stops people from building tornado shelters or strengthening their housing structures. The best period for preventive work is immediately after a disaster. Activity helps survivors get over recent horrors. A vigorous checking of building regulations, safety rules and evacuation procedures is usually conducted. Sometimes, fear of recurrence can lead to drastic action, like the removal of the remaining tips around Aberfan and the new flood prevention plans after the Florence deluge.

Disaster victims are not the only onces to feel strange sensations as they live through the devastating event. The problem of sightseers crowding in with apparently morbid interest in death and destruction is common to all large-scale catastrophes. The explanation of this relates back to that central emotion—isolation and abandonment. People watching a disaster have the satisfaction of seeing loneliness and despair hit *others:* as onlookers they can control their own deepseated fears of being lost, unable to cope and full of weakness. The childhood fear of being defenseless goes back to those moments when a baby screams in fright at being left alone or a toddler runs back to its mother after hearing a loud noise. Hundreds of other people jostling around him adds comfort and security to the sightseer's morbid enjoyment of the scene.

This element of feeling in control of the situation also explains the survivors who go wandering about, drinking in the sights as if trying to grasp the reality. Many families who pulled through the San Francisco earthquake drove downtown in carriages to look at the wreckage, unconcerned that greater destruction was overtaking the city in the form of fire.

It is possible that people are drawn to disaster areas in the way that they can be drawn to pornography. Sex and death are taboos in our society, and death is perhaps the greater unmentionable. There is a deep-seated fear of death in most people, and disasters are among the only respectable ways that people can indulge their curiosity. The fear of being weak and defenseless is the underlying fascination behind the horror of disasters. Prophets and moralists wag a finger and point out man's sin of pride in thinking he can master the universe and tame nature. The stories included here tell of epic attempts to harness natural forces and make full use of sea, land and air. Many of the disasters are, besides being evidence of man's bravery in the face of danger, a sharp reminder of human limitations. Only between 12 and 20 percent of individuals affected by a catastrophe function effectively in the aftermath. Most people are stunned and silent, unable to act. A disaster calls for strong natural leaders to help the majority to find a path back to usefulness and normality. Mass panic is a generally-expected concept that fascinates everyone, but one which rarely happens. The moment that friendship and co-operative activity begins, most human beings respond well and do their best to overcome the unexpected calamity.